"Kathy has beautifully woven an account of how the grace God so incredibly pours into us. She practically shares with us ways we can exhibit grace to others. You will be blessed by this book! I know I was."

—JENNIFER ROTHSCHILD, author of *Lessons I Learned in the Dark*; *Self Talk, Soul Talk*; and *God Is Just Not Fair: Finding Hope When Life Doesn't Make Sense* and founder of Fresh Grounded Faith events and womensministry.net

"Kathy Howard pinpoints what each of us needs—a fresh awareness of God's grace. Through the eyes of Paul, a self-claimed 'chief of sinners,' she helps us recognize, rest in, and share God's lavish grace."

—DEBBIE TAYLOR WILLIAMS, national Bible teacher and author of seven books, including, *If God is In Control, Why Am I a Basket Case?*

"The more I move through life, the more I recognize the unending, overwhelming need for grace in my relationship with God and others. Kathy Howard does more than point out our need for grace; she teaches us to not only pour it out, but also to lap it up. A must read for a needy world."

—KATHI LIPP, speaker and author of *Clutter Free*

"Kathy Howard's new book, *Lavish Grace*, had me at 'grace.' It's one of my heartbeat topics! And her book did not disappoint. You'll love how she deftly combines what Paul writes about grace with true-to-life application steps. She not only shares accounts of people from Bible times, but what people of today have faced as they learned to navigate the circumstances and character of grace in their own lives. The subtitle of the book is *poured out, poured through, and overflowing*. That's exactly how I've seen Kathy reflect a life of lavish grace—enough to share with others on their own grace journeys."

—KATHY CARLTON WILLIS, women's speaker, DVD Bible study presenter, and author of *Grin with Grace*

"Grace—that unearned, undeserved gift from God that washes over us each day as a follower of Christ. Kathy Howard helps us grasp the depth of this gift through a study of the life of the Apostle Paul and stories of women today who have personally experienced God's grace. Her 9-week interactive study will leave you with a deeper understanding of just how much God loves each of us as demonstrated through His gift of grace."

—WANDA LEE, executive director, National WMU®

"Grace is not a churchy, cliché topic that cleaned up, nice people sing about on Sundays from a hymnal. Instead, grace is the aggressive, offensive, complicated, and complete gift of Jesus that every soul has to contend with for both our eternal salvation and daily frustrations. God's love is not contingent on your goodness, and His forgiveness cannot be constrained by your rebellion. It's unsearchable. Impossible to comprehend, yet fully accessible and purposed to impact and inform the way you believe, live, and love others. *Lavish Grace* will help you navigate this critical dialog as the study takes you by the hand and leads you straight to God's Word. If you're ready to understand and embrace this life-altering love in a fresh way, then don't hesitate to take this grace-walk with Kathy."

—GWEN SMITH, speaker, worship leader, cofounder of Girlfriends in God, and author of *I Want It All* and *Broken into Beautiful*

"*Lavish Grace* is packed with powerful stories of changed lives. This Bible study explodes page after page with inspiration like, 'His grace is in such abundance we cannot hold it all. It overflows our ability to contain it.' What is this all about? How is grace able to remove guilt? Shame? Who is this God who gives us such grace? When you complete this book, you will understand the boundlessness of God's love from a new perspective. His rich outpouring of grace is the very foundation of God's salvation plan for us. Kathy Howard has put her whole heart into this book and shares a depth of knowledge of Scripture that will bless your heart."

—JONEAL KIRBY, author and founder of Heartfelt Ministries

"In *Lavish Grace*, Kathy Howard gives us wisdom, grace upon grace, by walking the reader through an accurate, life-changing, and practical view of God's rich, elaborate, extravagant, generous, and amazing grace! If you want to renew, revive, and rejuvenate your life with God's lavish grace, then the pages of this book will shower you with hope and help you embrace the exuberant, abundant, grace-filled life we all long for!"

—PAM FARREL, author of *7 Simple Skills for Every Woman: Success in Keeping It All Together* and *Men Are Like Waffles, Women Are Like Spaghetti*

LAVISH GRACE

POURED OUT, POURED THROUGH, *and* OVERFLOWING

KATHY HOWARD

OTHER NEW HOPE BOOKS
BY KATHY HOWARD

Before His Throne

Embraced by Holiness

Fed Up with Flat Faith

God's Truth Revealed

Unshakeable Faith

LAVISH GRACE

POURED OUT, POURED THROUGH, *and* OVERFLOWING

KATHY HOWARD

NEW HOPE® PUBLISHERS
Gospel-Centered. Missions-Driven.

BIRMINGHAM, ALABAMA

New Hope® Publishers
PO Box 12065
Birmingham, AL 35202-2065
NewHopePublishers.com
New Hope Publishers is a division of WMU®.

New Hope Publishers serves its authors as they express their views, which may not express the views of the publisher.

Library of Congress Cataloging-in-Publication Data

Names: Howard, Kathy, 1961- author.
Title: Lavish grace : poured out, poured through, and overflowing / Kathy Howard.
Description: Birmingham, AL : New Hope Publishers, 2016. | Includes bibliographical references.
Identifiers: LCCN 2016012885 | ISBN 9781625915030 (sc)
Subjects: LCSH: Grace (Theology)--Biblical teaching--Textbooks.
Classification: LCC BT761.3 .H69 2016 | DDC 234--dc23 LC record available at http://lccn.loc.gov/2016012885

ISBN-13: 978-1-62591-503-0

N174102 • 0816 • 2M1

To Janet, my precious sister-friend.
Both her life and her "home going"
exemplified the sufficiency and power of God's lavish grace.

I want to be just like her when I grow up.

CONTENTS

INTRODUCTION

FOR A LONG TIME I UNDERESTIMATED GOD'S GRACE. OH YES, I'VE KNOWN Ephesians 2:8–9 by memory since I was a girl:

> *For it is by grace you have been saved, through faith—and this is not from yourselves, it is the gift of God—not by works, so that no one can boast.*

But I mistakenly left God's grace on the altar of my conversion.

Then some serious trials and difficult challenges hit my life and I discovered my self-sufficiency was merely an illusion. I realized I couldn't live a day, make a move, or even fill my lungs with air without the glorious, ever-present grace of my great God.

His grace is always there. Sometimes it goes unnoticed. Sometimes it is rejected. But just as water is essential for physical life, God's grace is essential—and available—for my spiritual life.

Like a spring-fed river, divine grace flows constantly. Sometimes God's grace is quiet and deep, patiently soaking into the dry nooks and crannies of our souls. Other times it surges, cascades, and pounds, working to smooth our sharp edges and wash away deposits left behind by the world.

No dam can stop it. No bank can contain it. It knows no bounds.

The Apostle Paul understood God's grace in a way most of us never will. This man who persecuted and killed Jesus' followers received His grace in lavish abundance. Paul, the self-proclaimed "worst of sinners" (1 Timothy 1:16), experienced the overflowing richness of God's grace. And he was never the same.

Not only did Paul live his life as an expression of gratitude for God's unbounded grace, but a river of grace flows through his writings as well. In his letters, Paul shows how God's grace washes through and over every part of a believer's life. His grace is not "just enough" for us, and it's far more than "sufficient." It is freely given. Abundantly poured out. Without boundaries or limits.

As we study Paul's life and teachings together over the next nine weeks, we will see the extent and scope of God's grace for us—from His first *whispers of wooing* to our lives today.

Lavish Grace is a nine-week, interactive Bible study on Paul's experiences with and teachings on grace. It is designed to help you discover the riches and abundance of God's grace for yourself.

The nine weeks of study are evenly divided into three larger parts to help us grasp the depth and scope of God's grace:

1. GRACE POURED OUT—First, we'll see how our eternal salvation is completely and thoroughly a work of God's grace. From those first drawings of the Holy Spirit and our conversion, to our spiritual growth and service, His grace pours out to make us His own.

2. GRACE POURED THROUGH—Second, we'll discover how God calls us to be channels of His great grace, not just stagnant pools. How could we, who've received such glorious, undeserved grace, dare withhold it from others?

3. GRACE OVERFLOWING—Finally, we'll rejoice in the truth that God's grace is available for our every day and any day. In times of trials, struggles, and difficulties His grace bubbles up and overflows, supplying "immeasurably more" than we could "ask or imagine" (Ephesians 3:20).

Each week includes four sections. You can complete the entire lesson in one sitting or do a section a day for four days:

1. LEARNING IT—Paul experienced God's grace in abundance! Each week in this section, you'll see the effect of God's grace applied to the "worst of sinners."

2. TEACHING IT—Paul eloquently and profusely wrote and taught about what he himself had experienced—God's unbounded grace. In this section, you'll explore what Paul taught about the aspects of God's grace.

3. LIVING IT—No study of Scripture is complete without challenging ourselves to apply God's truth to our lives. This section will help you see how God wants to align your life to what you've learned.

4. GRACE APPLIED—These real-life stories highlight an aspect of God's grace experienced in the life of a contemporary woman. What she experienced just may help you!

I am honored to ride the river with you as we experience God's grace through our time of study together. May His lavish grace do its glorious work in your heart and life in the days ahead.

PART ONE

GRACE
POURED OUT

God's unbounded grace woos,
saves, calls, and grows!

My friend Katie met Sam at a Campus Crusade for Christ meeting during their first week at university. And she was impressed! Not only did Sam exhibit spiritual maturity and natural leadership skills, he was also handsome and a lot of fun to be around. Soon, they both accepted ministry responsibilities with Campus Crusade and began working together. Katie quickly decided Sam was the man for her. Unfortunately, Sam hadn't reached the same conclusion.

Over the next few years, Sam and Katie continued to spend a lot of time around each other through their ministries with Campus Crusade. They developed a strong friendship, but Katie longed for more. So she decided to help Sam along, to woo him with her sweet attention.

Since the way to a man's heart is through his stomach, Katie baked cookies for Sam. She regularly managed to run into him as they both crossed campus on their way to classes. Katie used her artistic talent to create a special drawing of a bird with a passage from Ephesians. She also gave him other gifts that reminded him of their mutual love for Jesus, like a hymnal and cross-stitched Scripture. Katie appealed to Sam's fun side by mailing him a pumpkin through the campus post office. One summer Katie even traveled to visit Sam in another state where he was doing short-term ministry.

However, more than all these demonstrations of affection, Katie prayed for Sam. Katie also prayed for herself. She asked God to take away her desire for Sam if the longing was not from Him.

The summer before Katie graduated, she and Sam were both members of a group doing missions work in the Philippines. For the first nine weeks they were assigned to the same team, but during the last week they were put on different ones. The distance and separation caught Sam's attention. With Katie no longer right there, he realized the hole her absence left in his life. A new desire awakened in Sam's heart. A year later Sam proposed.

God permanently put Sam and Katie on the same team. They committed themselves to each other and to God. More than three decades later they're still doing life—and ministry—together. Katie chose Sam for herself from the beginning. But it took years of wooing and waiting for Sam to reach the same decision.

It's the same between God and us. He chose us for Himself long before we were even aware of Him. He chose to love us when we were indifferent to His love. He offered His grace even while we were still rebellious. In Week One of our study together, we'll explore the incredible truth that God woos us with whispers of His grace so we will chose Him, too. Get ready to rejoice over the glorious and gracious wooing of our Savior!

LEARNING IT

God's grace is radical. Extreme. Counterintuitive. He pours it out on those who don't deserve it. God lavishes His grace on those who aren't even seeking it. He even generously extends it to those who hate Him and persecute His people.

Saul of Tarsus fit that description. In the years immediately following the death and resurrection of Jesus, Saul was the archenemy of Jesus' followers. He did everything "possible to oppose the name of Jesus" (Acts 26:9). He went from synagogue to synagogue to punish Jews who "belonged to the Way" (Acts 9:2). He traveled from city to city to arrest them and put them in chains. He zealously and violently sought them out and put them to death. And he did it all with the blessing and backing of the Jewish rulers.

Saul was a strict Pharisee, a brilliant young lawyer educated in Jerusalem under the great teacher Gamaliel (Acts 22:3). Saul was an insider, no doubt privy to much of the same information as the highest echelon of Jewish leadership.

Yet even while Saul breathed out murderous threats against believers, God wooed him with His grace. Years later, in his letter to the Christians in Galatia, Saul (Paul) acknowledged God had "set me apart from my mother's womb and called me by his grace" (Galatians 1:15). Have you ever wondered how God worked in Saul's heart and mind before his encounter with Jesus on the road to Damascus? Saul obviously felt threatened by the gospel message of Christ. That's why he worked so hard to stop it. But the signs of God's grace flowing all around Saul were not without effect. They prepared him for a life-changing meeting on a dusty road.

Read the following passages, and write down every sign you see of God's grace at work. Remember that Saul would have known what was happening with this strange new "Jewish cult." Saul was probably in attendance at Peter and John's hearing before the Sanhedrin. (Feel free to scan the lengthier passages if time is a factor.)

Acts 2:42–47

Acts 3:1–10

Acts 4:1–22

Acts 5:12–16

Acts 5:17–42

Imagine the charged atmosphere in Jerusalem and how it probably affected Saul. Everyone was talking about Jesus and His followers. People joined their ranks daily. They healed the lame, exorcised demons, and performed other miraculous signs and wonders. Peter and John walked right out of a locked prison. The believers made such an impact some of the priests even joined them!

Saul probably heard Peter's Spirit-filled testimony. He heard the gospel message loud and clear (Acts 3:1–26; 4:1–22). In his book, *Paul: A Man of Grace and Grit,* Charles Swindoll reflects on this moment:

> While standing in the shadows listening to Peter speak, the hair on the back of his neck bristled. This young, pious Pharisee, a Hebrew of Hebrews, listened angrily as the ignorant fisherman named Peter spoke of the now-dead Jesus who claimed to be God. It was almost more than he could bear. Passion boiled within him as Saul began formulating plans, thinking, *If I could just get my hands on him, I'd kill him like all the rest.* Little did he

know this "ignorant fisherman" would be his co-laborer in the work of establishing Christian churches throughout the known world.

The council wanted to kill Peter and John, but ironically, Gamaliel, Saul's mentor, intervened.

Read Acts 5:33–40. Why did Gamaliel advise the council to release Peter and John?

How do you imagine Saul felt about this?

After Peter and John's release from prison, the number of disciples continued to increase dramatically. As their numbers grew, the church chose seven men to serve as deacons to minister to the widows among them. One of these deacons was Stephen. And Stephen became a target for Saul.

Read Acts 6:5–10. Based on the passage, briefly describe Stephen's character.

Read Acts 6:11–15, and mark the following statements as TRUE or FALSE.

❏ T ❏ F   The Jews who argued with Stephen secretly recruited false witnesses against him.

❏ T ❏ F   They forced Stephen to appear before the Sanhedrin.

☐ T ☐ F   Stephen testified against Moses and the law.
☐ T ☐ F   Stephen's face looked like an angel's.

As Stephen answered the false charges against him (Acts 7:1–53), his face was "like the face of an angel" (Acts 6:15). Every member of the Sanhedrin saw it. Everyone gathered to hear Stephen's testimony saw it. Saul saw it.

Well, I don't know about you, but I've never seen an angel's face. (That I know of anyway!) So, what does that mean? What was so significant about Stephen's appearance? *Book of Acts: An Introduction and Commentary* explains it this way:

> The description is of a person who is close to God and reflects some of his glory as a result of being in his presence (Ex. 34:29ff). It is a divine vindication of Stephen, and an indication of his inspiration to make his defence (sic).

The Sanhedrin and everyone gathered there recognized that Stephen had a unique, intimate relationship with God. His very appearance proved the truth of his testimony. Yet they would not yield to the ultimate truth—that they had betrayed and murdered the Messiah they'd been waiting for (Acts 7:51–53). Instead they reacted with murderous fury.

☞ Read the account of Stephen's martyrdom in Acts 7:54–60 and 8:1, and answer the following questions.

Who does the passage make a point of telling us was present? What was he doing?

In what ways do you think God could have used Stephen's testimony and death to impact Saul?

Saul was present at the stoning of Stephen. He not only "approved" it, he may have even instigated it. But that doesn't mean God didn't use it as a stepping stone in Saul's journey toward Jesus. In fact, God often works like that.

☞ Review the questions in the "Learning It" section. Make a bulleted list of the workings of God's grace Saul witnessed in Jerusalem.

We may not see outward evidence of God's wooing of Saul at this point in his life, but God surely had his attention. Even a quick look at Saul's (Paul's) letters reveals he understood God was wooing him with grace while he was still a rebellious sinner.

TEACHING IT

My friend Chelsey used to think people who believed in God were stupid. She viewed them as weak, simply clinging to myths to get through life. That was easy to believe as long as her life was easy. But when things got difficult and she had nowhere to turn, she ended up in a destructive pattern of partying and drugs.

But in the place Chelsey describes as "empty, dark, and loveless," God's grace flowed. First, He helped her break the hold of addiction. Then He moved Chelsey next door to Amber, a young Christian mom who befriended her. Initially, Chelsey considered Amber a "Bible thumper." But when she realized Amber's life was firmly grounded in something special, Chelsey embraced the friendship.

Months later, when Amber invited Chelsey to attend her ladies Bible study group, Chelsey accepted. At first, her motivation was simply to live a better life; she was still skeptical about the existence of God. But God was working in her heart and mind. By the time the study ended several weeks later, Chelsey had given her life to Jesus.

Chelsey was rebellious and rejected God's truth. She did not seek God on her own, but God sought her. Chelsey's story is our story. The details may be different, but the themes are the same. Let's see how Paul taught these truths.

Read Romans 3:9–12. Check any of the following statements that accurately reflect Paul's teaching in this passage.

❑ Every single person has sinned.

❑ No one seeks after God.

❑ Everyone has turned away from God.

Yes, Paul received these truths from divine inspiration, but he also knew them from experience. He had not sought after God. He turned away from God and even persecuted His people. Yet in His grace, God sought Paul.

Read Galatians 1:11–17. What was Paul doing when God called him "by his grace?"

When did God choose Paul for Himself?

While Paul was zealously trying to annihilate the Church, God was pursuing him. While Paul had his heart set on destruction, God had His heart set on Paul. And, sister, the same is true in our lives. When we were still running hard away from God, He pursued us with His grace. Doesn't that just bowl you over?

Read Ephesians 1:3–14.

The Greek word translated as "grace" in Ephesians 1:6 and 7, is *chàris*. Here are some of the facets of God's grace based on the definition of *chàris* from *The Complete Word Study New Testament*:
- Closely related to the Greek word we translate as "joy"
- Favor, kindness, acceptance
- Favor bestowed on the undeserving without expectation of return
- Absolute freeness of God's loving-kindness to men
- Motivated by the bounty and heart of the Giver
- Unearned and unmerited favor
- Forgives sin and affects a person's sinful nature, shaping her to be used for God's good purposes
- Results in joy and gratitude in the one who receives it

🖙 Slowly read back through the definition of God's grace above. Underline any aspect of grace that is new to you. Write a summary definition of grace in the space below.

Ephesians 1:3–14 is all one long sentence in the Greek. Once Paul started praising God he didn't stop to take a breath for 12 verses! It reminds me of an excited young child who wants so much to tell you everything; she doesn't even slow down enough to breathe. I can see Paul bursting with excitement and joy over what God has done.

☞ Look back over verses 3–14. List every word or phrase you find in the passage that describes God's actions toward us.

When did God decide to act in these ways toward us? (See verse 4.)

Before God created the heavens and the earth, He chose to love you. He desired to make you His own, even before there was time. And He put a plan in place to make it possible. Before you ever knew you needed a Savior, the Father determined Jesus would be your eternal hope. Then with His lavish grace, He wooed you.

LIVING IT

It's time to make the truths we've learned this week personal. They aren't just true in Paul's life or the lives of believers in general. They're true in my life—and your life.

Read John 6:44, and rewrite it in your own words below. Make it personal by using your name.

Read Jeremiah 31:3, and check below the manner in which God chooses to draw—or woo—you.
- ❏ With brute force
- ❏ With pleading and threats
- ❏ With everlasting love and loving kindness

🕊 Think about your own life before salvation. In what ways did God draw you? How did He work around and in your life to reveal Himself to you?

Throughout Scripture, God is the Initiator. Even in the Garden when Adam and Eve disobeyed God and sin entered the world, God sought the sinner. (See Genesis 3:8–9.) While we were still His enemies, God proved His love to us in the most radical way. "But God showed his great love for us by sending Christ to die for us while we were still sinners" (Romans 5:8 NLT).

Read John 12:32–33. What ultimate act of grace does God use to draw us to Himself?

The Heavenly Father draws us to the Cross of Christ because there—and only there—can His grace be applied. The Cross is the "grace point," the place where God's justice and mercy meet.

Next week we will take a closer look at God's grace in our salvation, but let's dwell on this truth for a moment: We do not deserve salvation. We are not worthy of a relationship with God. Yet, He chooses to love us. He chooses to extend His grace and makes it possible by His own sacrifice. By definition, God's grace flows from *His* heart. It's based on *His* bounty, *His* character. We do not merit His grace. We cannot earn it. Yet in His loving-kindness He woos us to Himself and freely pours out His grace through the death of His Son.

After our conversion, on the born again side, God still woos us. Through times of rebellion, complacency, grief, and struggle, God gently draws us back to Himself with cords of love. He will not let us go. He calls us from our wanderings. He longs to protect us from pain of our own making.

🖎 Perhaps you are in a time of spiritual wandering right now. Stop for a moment and ask God to evaluate your heart. Is He wooing you back from any of the following?

❑ Unconfessed sin

❑ Rebellious attitude

❑ Complacency in your relationship with Him

❑ Disconnect from His people

❑ Lack of service or ministry

❑ Other

Will you respond to His grace today?

Thank God for His unbounded grace in your life. Write a brief prayer of thanksgiving.

GRACE APPLIED

AUTHOR'S NOTE: *It's often helpful to see timeless spiritual truths demonstrated in someone's life. At the end of each week, you'll find a story about God's lavish grace generously poured out into the life of one of His children. Read the story, then answer the questions designed to help you apply these truths to your own life.*

Cathy learned to love Jesus and the community of God's people when she was just a girl. Raised by Christian parents, she spent her childhood connected to the church. But she was merely participating in religion. She lacked a true relationship with Jesus. Looking back though, Cathy can see the thread of God's grace running through those years.

Not long after Cathy married Don, her high school sweetheart, they moved to the Virgin Islands for a few years of adventure. Hungry for a community of faith, they readily accepted an invitation from a neighbor to visit the Bible study group he attended.

Don and Cathy felt welcomed and comfortable there. The people demonstrated a strong commitment to their faith. Their values and morality matched what Cathy knew growing up. But, neither Don nor Cathy had a solid foundation in key biblical truths. They weren't prepared to stand against the false teaching of the group. Soon, they were deeply entrenched in a cult.

When Cathy became pregnant, she and Don moved back to their hometown. Still members of the religious cult, Don and Cathy attempted to share their new beliefs with their family. Cathy's mom, who had a solid, dynamic relationship with Jesus, loved them unconditionally and prayed constantly.

A couple of years later when Cathy had a serious health scare with a tubal pregnancy, it raised questions for Don and he began searching the Bible. God brought godly Christian men across his path and started the process of replacing false teaching with His truth. But when Don left their faith, Cathy refused to go with him.

WEEK 1

31

The new divide in Don and Cathy's faith rocked their marriage. Their home was filled with constant tension and frequent arguments. He took their two daughters to church while Cathy continued to go to the cult gatherings. But when Cathy went to see a lawyer, Don called a truce. If Cathy would agree to be open to God showing her truth, Don would stop fighting her.

Over the next few months, Cathy developed a friendship with a neighbor named Anita. Conversations began to turn to spiritual topics. They often talked about Scripture. Cathy shared her understanding and Anita shared hers. Slowly, God washed away the lies Cathy had believed. He renewed her mind with His truth.

At 27 years old, Cathy gave her life to Jesus, and God made her His own. From the time she was a child, through Satan's lies, and into the light of truth, God continued to draw her to Himself. His grace never let go.

Make a list of ways you read of God's grace working in Cathy's life, drawing her to Himself.

How did God use other people in Cathy's faith journey?

Think about your life before salvation. How was God at work in your life
even then? Write the names of people God used along the way.

Has God crossed your path with anyone who is still "on their way" to
God? Who is it? How might God want to use you in their life?

WEEK TWO: GRACE LAND
GRACE NOTE: OUR SALVATION—FROM BEGINNING TO
END—IS A WORK OF GOD'S GRACE.

Growing up, Judy rarely went to church. Her widowed mother worked two jobs to provide for the family—it simply didn't fit their crazy schedule. But Judy's hardworking mom modeled a solid work ethic and strong values for her daughter. So, as a young adult, Judy considered herself a decent, responsible, "good" person.

Judy married a man from a strong Christian family. Randy's job moved them frequently, so church attendance was not a high priority during the early years of their marriage. But God was working. For example, whenever Judy and Randy got together with his parents, they always told her about the grace and love of Jesus. Judy heard the gospel, but it had not yet penetrated her heart.

Then five years into marriage, Randy was transferred to Florida. As God would have it, they moved right next door to a Christian woman named Peggy. She invited Judy to join her Bible study group, but Judy wasn't ready yet.

Over several months a solid friendship developed between the two women. Judy grew to trust and respect Peggy. So when Peggy asked again, Judy accepted her invitation to the Bible study group.

The pastor of the church led the study. The very first week he talked about sin and every individual's need for a Savior. He shared verses from the Bible about the nature of sin, the fact that every person is a sinner, and how our sin separates us from our holy God.

Most of what the pastor said was new to Judy. At first, she thought it simply didn't apply to her. After all, she was truly a "good" person. But as he continued to teach from the Bible, God quietly spoke truth to her heart. Judy realized she was indeed a sinner. She could never be good enough on her own. She needed a Savior!

Judy remembers her feelings the day God saved her. "I knew I had to make a decision. I accepted the atoning blood of Christ on the Cross to cover my sins. God reconciled me to Him forever. He awakened my heart!"

Judy began her life with Jesus at the age of 25. That day, the "good girl" became a redeemed sinner. Ever since, her life has been a constant quest for more of Him.

LEARNING IT

Saul's story of conversion may be more "dramatic" than Judy's, but neither of them deserved God's saving grace. Neither could ever be good enough to earn eternal salvation. Their salvation—and ours— is solely an act of God's grace.

Before we take a closer look at Saul's moment of conversion, let's paint a colorful "before" portrait. Read the following passages, and then write words and phrases that describe Saul before Jesus saved him.

Acts 8:1–3

Acts 9:1–2

Acts 22:2–8

Acts 26:9–11

Galatians 1:13–14

Do you have a solid picture of Saul the persecutor in your mind? His main goal in life, his primary focus, was to completely and permanently eradicate the people of The Way. And he would use whatever means possible to succeed. This man would never come to Jesus unless God acted first. Yes, this man's salvation would require a radical, divine intervention of grace.

Read Acts 9:1–3, and briefly answer the following questions.

Where was Saul going and why?

Who initiated this "mission"?

Describe Saul's attitude as he began this journey.

At what point in the journey did Jesus intercept Saul?

The Syrian city of Damascus was about 150 miles north of Jerusalem and had a large Jewish population. Saul knew he would find many Jewish "traitors" there who believed Jesus of Nazareth was the only way to Jehovah. According to the *Book of Acts: An Introduction and Commentary*, their claim of knowing the absolute way of salvation earned Christians the name "those of the Way." Saul would do everything in his power to put a permanent stop to their heresy. So, armed with authority from the high priest and bolstered by murderous intent, Saul stormed down to Damascus. But near the end of his journey—without any warning—the glory of Jesus exploded all around him.

Read Acts 9:4–9, and briefly answer the following questions.

What question did Jesus ask Saul?

How did Jesus identify Himself?

What did Jesus tell Saul to do?

What was the physical result of Saul's encounter with Jesus?

Read Acts 5:33–39, which we read last week. In what way does Gamaliel's statement in verse 39 apply to Saul?

Saul's entire world was turned upside down. Everything he so zealously believed, his life's mission, had just been shattered. Jesus was *not* dead. In the light of the glory of the resurrected Christ, Saul saw himself for what he was. A murderer. A raging madman who fought against God and slaughtered His people. The chief of sinners.

Read Acts 26:12–18, and answer the following questions. (This passage records Paul's own testimony, given about 20 years later, to King Agrippa while in prison in Caesarea.)

Why did Jesus say He appeared to Paul?

What did Jesus say He would do for Paul?

What would Paul do under the authority and power of Jesus?

In Acts 26:14, Paul recalled these words of Jesus: "Saul, Saul, why do you persecute me? It is hard for you to kick against the goads." A goad was a slender, pointed stick farmers used to prod a stubborn ox. If the ox kicked out against the goad in resistance, its sharp point would stab its leg. Fighting the goad caused self-inflicted pain. Jesus' use of this common expression shows Jesus had been "prodding" Saul for some time. Last week, we looked at some of the ways Jesus wooed Saul with displays of His grace. But Saul had stubbornly resisted.

☞ Now read Acts 9:10–19 for the rest of Saul's conversion story. Scripture doesn't tell us, but why do you think God may have allowed Saul to experience three days of physical blindness?

Saul's three-day fast indicates he spent this time in prayer and repentance. Saul didn't deserve God's forgiveness. Yet, Jesus had a plan for him. He could never earn redemption. Yet, God poured out His grace in abundance. The man who had been both physically and spiritually blind received his sight!

Read 1 Timothy 1:12–17. Check any of the following statements that are true.
❑ Paul considered himself unworthy of forgiveness and salvation.
❑ God's abundant grace wrought a radical transformation in Paul's life.
❑ Paul's salvation stands as an example of the unbounded nature of God's grace.

Did you hear Paul's overwhelming gratitude to God for the outpouring of His grace? God saved "the worst of sinners" as a demonstration of His mercy, unlimited patience, and unbounded grace. God lovingly wooed this violent man and appointed him to His service.

Charles Swindoll reflected on Paul's gratitude in *Paul: A Man of Grace and Grit*:

He hated the name of Jesus. So much so, he became a self-avowed, violent aggressor, persecuting and killing Christians in allegiance to the God of heaven. Shocking though it may seem, we must never forget the pit from which he came. The better we understand the darkness of his past, the more we will understand his gratitude for grace.

TEACHING IT

A couple of years ago, my car battery died and left me stranded in a doctor's office parking lot. I didn't get a warning. I had no trouble starting the car to drive to the appointment, but when I came out to go home, the motor didn't even try to start.

I intercepted a cowboy headed out to his pickup truck and asked for his help. He agreed to do what he could and managed to finagle his vehicle into a position to connect our batteries. But still my car wouldn't start.

I decided it must be something other than the battery. Maybe the starter. So I called for roadside assistance and my father-in-law. The tow truck took my car to the dealership and my father-in-law took me home.

Later that day the service department called with the diagnosis. It was the battery. *What?* I asked why the "jump" didn't get it going. According to the man who understands cars far more than I do, a battery has to have at least some life left in it to respond to a jump. My battery, on the other hand, didn't have a single spark of life remaining. The only hope left for my car was a brand new battery. One that contained life. So, dead battery out and live battery in. Car started. Amazing.

Before Christ saves us, we're like my car sitting in the doctor's office parking lot. We might look fine from the outside, but in reality we're dead. Paul emphasized this truth in his letter to the Christians in Ephesus.

Read Ephesians 2:1. Now fill in the following blank from the New Living Translation:

Once you were _____ because of your disobedience and your many sins.

The Greek word translated "dead" is *nekrós*. *The Complete Word Study New Testament* defines it this way:

> Spiritual death, dead in sin, separated from the vivifying grace of God, or more distinctly, having one's soul separated from the enlivening influences of the divine light and spirit . . . and consequently having no hope of eternal life.

☞ Read Romans 3:23 and 6:23 to answer the following questions.

Who has sinned?

Does that include you?

What is the result of your sin?

Spiritual death cuts us off completely from the source of spiritual life. We have no power to save ourselves, and no access to the One who does. Sounds like a hopeless state, doesn't it? Oh, but the grace of God . . .

☞ Read Ephesians 2:1–22 without stopping so you can feel the impact of God's grace at work. Then go back through the chapter using the following table to record words, phrases, and facts that describe the two spiritual conditions—dead and alive.

DEAD	G R A C E	ALIVE

We've looked at the meaning of "dead," specifically spiritual death; now let's take a closer look at spiritual "life."

Read Ephesians 4:18. From what are we separated when we are spiritually dead?

The Greek word translated "life" in Ephesians 4:18 is zōē. According to *Vine's Complete Expository Dictionary*, zōē is "life in the absolute sense, life as God has it, that which the Father has in Himself, and which He gave to the Incarnate Son to have in Himself."

☞ Now let's pull this together. Read the following passages, which all contain zōē, or one of its variations, and record what you learn about true, spiritual life.

1 John 1:2

1 John 5:11–13

John 5:24–26

I'm having serious trouble staying in my chair as I write this. I am so overwhelmed by what God has done for us in Christ! Did you see it? God replaces our death with His Life. And His Life is Jesus Himself. Eternal life is *The Life* in us.

In her book *Power in the Blood of Christ*, Jennifer Kennedy Dean elaborates on this truth:

> Eternal life is a completely new life—the life of Jesus. It is not an addendum tacked on to my earth-life. Eternal life is not something God gives me apart from Himself. He is eternal life and He is in me. When He transfused

me with His life, at that very moment I received eternal life. I'm living it right now. Some day I will live my eternal life without the limits of an earth-body, but the life will be the same.

We find the heart of God's eternal salvation in Ephesians 2:4–5:

> *But because of his great love for us, God, who is rich in mercy, made us alive with Christ even when we were dead in transgressions—it is by grace you have been saved.*

Christ's death paid our sin debt and reconciled us to God. Christ's life in us is our eternal salvation. We have been joined with Him. God's work through Christ is His work in us. Our new life in Christ is really Christ's life in us!

We were dead. God extended grace. We are alive because Christ lives in us. Now that's amazing grace.

LIVING IT

Are you dead or alive? Has there ever been a time in your life when you received God's unbounded grace and crossed over from death to life?

Let's take a quick run down Paul's "Roman Road." Read the passages below and rewrite the primary truth in your own words.

Romans 3:23

Romans 3:10–11

Romans 6:23

Romans 5:8

Romans 10:9–10

Romans 5:1

Romans 8:1

Now reread Ephesians 2:8–9, which you read in the previous section.

Have you crossed from death to life through faith by God's grace?
Circle one: Yes   No

If you circled "no," then why not today? You can't do anything to earn God's great salvation. You just need to realize your need and receive His gift of grace.

• Acknowledge you are a sinner and in need of a Savior.
• Believe that Jesus Christ died to pay the debt for your sins and rose from the grave victorious.
• Confess with your mouth that Jesus Christ is Lord!

If you made this decision for the first time, welcome to the family of God! If you have been a believer for some time, more than likely there is someone in your life you think God won't—or "can't" save.

Maybe this person is totally resistant to the things of God. Maybe she lives a depraved life. God's grace is more than sufficient—look at Paul's life.

☞ Go back and read the character description of Saul you wrote last week. If anyone "couldn't" be saved, it was Saul. Yet God saved him. How should this realization affect the way you pray for others? The way you share the gospel?

Maybe there is something in your past you feel is beyond the scope of God's grace. Think about this in light of what we've studied this week. Will you accept that God's grace is more than sufficient?

GRACE APPLIED

Laverne describes her life before Jesus as "filled with guilt and fear." Raised in a traditionally religious home, she attended Catholic school for 12 years. She knew about God and she knew church doctrine. Laverne even knew about the Crucifixion. But she didn't hear about salvation through faith in Jesus or the message of God's grace until years later.

After college graduation, Laverne took a job teaching school in Montana. She uses the term "ungodly" to describe that time—not because her lifestyle was highly immoral, but simply because she lived without any regard for God.

However her Catholic upbringing still had a strong influence in her life. Late night partying with friends followed by early morning

Mass and confession became a regular pattern. "I constantly felt guilty," Laverne said. "I feared God would grab me up and throw me into the dregs of hell."

More than a decade later, God graciously began to draw Laverne to Jesus. By this time, she was married, living in California, and mother to two "hyperactive" children. Her husband Denny had been transferred to Texas, but Laverne and the kids were waiting until the end of the school year to join him.

Laverne was overwhelmed with the kids, the changes, and selling a house with her husband away. She needed help. Laverne was ready to hear from God. And God began to speak, to gently woo her.

One night, Laverne listened to Billy Graham. One thing he said grabbed her attention and wouldn't let go. "People are so sinful, they don't even blush." She wondered why that statement bothered her so. After all, she had never done anything really bad like killing someone.

A few days later, a woman knocked on her door. She began the conversation by asking Laverne a question: "Are you a Christian?" Laverne didn't even respond, she simply turned away and slammed the door. But the question continued to echo in her mind. Laverne realized she didn't even know what it meant to be a Christian.

Sin. Salvation. Guilt. Fear. Laverne's thoughts and emotions reached a breaking point. She believed God existed. She knew about Jesus and His death on the Cross. But she also knew she wasn't saved. Laverne was ready to surrender her life to God. When she cried out to Him, He heard, and responded with His saving grace.

"I am in awe of it always. I was so filled with joy, something I'd never experienced before. My anxiety was gone. I had a transformation."

Laverne began to devour the Bible. She canceled everything on her calendar so she could stay home and read it all day. She listened to faith-based radio programs and began going to a weekly discipleship class at a church close to her home. Looking back, Laverne knows God was preparing her to teach others.

Denny, though surprised with Laverne's newfound faith, never hindered her pursuit of Jesus. However, for a while he teasingly referred to her as a "Jesus freak."

I met Laverne about five years ago when my husband and I moved to a new city.

She is a great-grandmother, Jesus freak, and dynamo all wrapped up in one petite, little package. She loves God's Word and has a passion for teaching and discipleship. Laverne particularly likes to teach about God's grace. Those days of guilt and fear are long gone.

Describe how guilt characterized Laverne's life before salvation. How did guilt affect her daily life?

Did you ever struggle with guilt before God saved you? What makes it possible for believers to live "guilt-free?"

Through a series of events and people, God intercepted Laverne with His grace and brought her from death to life. What was the turning point for you? Describe the moment when God brought you from death to life.

Laverne's new life in Christ was immediately marked by a strong desire for God's Word. Think back to your early days of salvation. List some of the changes God made in you right away.

Before Jesus saved Stephanie, she jumped from one painful experience or foolish choice to the next. Pregnant at 17, she married her baby's father, but by 19 Stephanie was a single mom. Desperate for love, she hit the bar scene and soon met a handsome drummer. They fell in love and married, but their life together revolved around rock and roll, bars, and the next gig.

Stephanie felt desperate and needy, but she honestly didn't know what she lacked until God lovingly reached out and began to draw her close. Stephanie's journey to Jesus began when she heard the gospel message for the first time from a television evangelist. For the next two years, God wooed Stephanie, showing her His unconditional love. Finally, she yielded to that love and gave her life to Jesus.

Stephanie immediately longed to know more about this God who saved her. As she immersed herself in Bible study, Stephanie's passion for God's Word deepened. Over time, this passion developed into a longing to share God's Word with everyone who would listen.

Stephanie knew God had a purpose for her life. She strongly sensed His call to share with others what God had given her. "My calling—which the Lord put on my heart not long after my salvation—is to reach others with God's message of salvation and teach them to know and obey His Word. Reach them and teach them."

Over the years, God showed Stephanie how to obey that calling in specific ways. He refined and focused her ministry, making the most of the wisdom and experience she gained through all the circumstances of her life. Stephanie learned that God doesn't waste anything He allows into our lives. If we let Him, He can and will graciously use even the ugliest and most painful things for His glory.

For instance, Stephanie has a vast range of experiences. Teen mom. Divorced. Single mom. Blended family. Married mom without Jesus. Christian mom with an unsaved husband. One family united under Christ. God used this life journey to shape Stephanie for a unique purpose.

Today, Stephanie leads a growing ministry that mobilizes, trains, and equips churches and individuals to change the world for Jesus by mentoring mothers. This ministry reaches women who know Christ and those who don't yet know Him.

God uniquely prepared Stephanie and specifically called her to mentor mothers.

You also have unique life experiences, passions, and gifts God wants to use for His glory. Just like Stephanie, and just like Paul, God saved you to a specific purpose. This purpose is another work of His grace in your life. Are you living it?

LEARNING IT

In last week's lesson, we discovered that God saved us *from* death and *into* life. He graciously saved us *from* the bondage of sin and an eternity separated *from* Him. He saved us *from* eternal condemnation. Oh, praise be to God, He saved us *from*!

But God didn't merely save us *from* something horrible; He also saved us *into* something glorious. By His grace, God saved us *into* a life-giving relationship with Jesus. He saved us *into* spiritual freedom. He saved us *into* an eternity in His presence. And He saved us *into* a new life marked by unique purpose and ministry.

Sometimes, as believers, we get hung up on the "from" of our salvation. While looking back does help foster gratitude for all God has done, we also need to follow Paul's example and purposefully move forward in God's grace to service and ministry.

🖎 Read Galatians 1:11–17. What was Saul doing before his encounter with Jesus on the Damascus road?

🖎 What was God's plan for Saul?

Saul's salvation—this complete change of life direction—took him by surprise. Saul had plans. With the right education and pedigree, he quickly rose in the ranks of Judaism. Saul's future as a prominent religious leader looked certain.

But God had different plans. In one bright moment on a dusty road to Damascus, the God of the universe pulled the proverbial rug from under the feet of Saul of Tarsus. This rising star of Jewish religious life, now lay humbly at the feet of the One he had persecuted. God chose Saul from birth. By His grace, God saved Saul from eternal death. And by His grace, God saved Saul into a specific purpose and ministry.

🖎 Read the following passages. Beside each one, record what you learn about God's specific purpose for Saul and his call to ministry.

Acts 9:15–16

Acts 23:11

Acts 26:12–20

Ephesians 3:2–9

Look back at Ephesians 3:2–9. List the familiar words and phrases Paul used to describe this purpose God gave him. (See verses 2, 7, and 8.)

God's grace did not end at Paul's conversion. Paul understood that God's calling to ministry was also a work of grace in his life. God not only called Paul to a unique ministry, He also graciously prepared him to be able to carry out the task. Paul considered both the ministry and the preparation gracious gifts from God.

🖙 Read Acts 21:37–40 and 22:1–28, paying particular attention to 21:37; 22:1–3; and 22:21–28. (Note: A Roman commander had arrested Paul in Jerusalem after some Jews in the Temple incited a mob against him. God used this incident to begin Paul's journey to Rome.) Also read

Philippians 3:4–6. Use the information in these passages to make a list of facts about Paul's background, experience, and education.

In several places, including Acts 22:3, the Bible records that Paul was born in Tarsus. *Eerdmans Dictionary of the Bible* records the city's population as half a million people who largely valued culture, learning, and philosophy. We don't know exactly when Paul left Tarsus and moved to Jerusalem, but this decidedly Roman city left its mark on Paul and his family.

Some scholars think Paul left Tarsus for Jerusalem during his teen years, but many believe the construction of Acts 22:3 tells us Paul was taken to Jerusalem at a very early age. According to I. Howard Marshal in the *Book of Acts: An Introduction and Commentary,* it is likely that Paul was born to Jewish parents living in Tarsus, moved while he was young, and spent his formative years in Jerusalem. Since Paul was born a Roman citizen, his Jewish father would have also been a citizen. Although we don't know how this happened, it greatly benefited Paul.

Paul received his rabbinic education under the teacher Gamaliel, a Pharisee and member of the Sanhedrin. According to *Eerdmans Dictionary of the Bible*, Gamaliel "focused on the importance of study and the teacher-student relationship." He was "quite tolerant of Gentiles" and made sure his students studied Greek.

☞ Now reread Acts 9:15. God told Ananias that Paul was His "chosen instrument to proclaim my name to the Gentiles and their kings and to the people of Israel." Using the facts you discovered in the last question and the additional information in the paragraphs above, use the following table to describe how God could work through Paul's unique background, experience, and education to take Jesus' name to each group.

FACTS ABOUT PAUL	GENTILES	KINGS	PEOPLE OF ISRAEL

In His sovereignty, God gave Paul the experiences, education, and background he needed to carry out his ministry call. Paul spoke both Greek and Aramaic fluently, so he could easily speak to both Jews and Gentiles. Having thoroughly experienced both cultures, he was comfortable in both Jewish and Roman surroundings. And since only Roman citizens could appeal to Caesar, Paul's Roman citizenship paved the way for him to preach the gospel in Rome. (See Acts 25:9–12.)

According to Acts 26:19–20, did Paul obey God's call? Circle one:

Yes   No   Partially

Paul faithfully obeyed God and fulfilled the unique purpose designed for him. He boldly proclaimed the name of Jesus in synagogues around the Roman kingdom and before a hostile Jewish crowd in Jerusalem. He declared the gospel message of salvation to Gentiles from Damascus to Rome. And he held out the words of life to governors, kings, and perhaps even Caesar himself. Saul the persecutor, transformed by the grace of God, became Paul the Apostle. "Not disobedient to the vision from heaven" (Acts 26:19), he carried the name of Jesus to "the Gentiles and their kings and to the people of Israel" (Acts 9:15).

TEACHING IT

Even before his salvation, God worked through Paul's life to prepare him for a unique purpose. After his conversion, Paul committed to learning and spiritual growth to better equip himself to carry out his calling. Although the information about Paul's first years as a believer is sparse, Scripture gives us enough to piece together a brief picture:

- Traveled from Damascus to Arabia (Galatians 1:17)—Many scholars feel this trip may have been a time of spiritual retreat for Paul, to reconcile everything he knew from the Old Testament Scriptures with his new reality in Christ. To immerse himself in the reality and presence of his Savior. To soak in His grace.
- Returned to Damascus (Galatians 1:17, Acts 9:19–23)—Still learning and growing, Paul immediately obeyed God's call by preaching Christ to the Jews in Damascus. Eventually, in order to escape a murder plot, he had to flee the city.
- Brief visit to Jerusalem (Acts 9:26–29, Galatians 1:18–20)—Three years passed between Paul's conversion and his first trip back to Jerusalem. He spent two weeks "getting acquainted" with Peter. According to *The Expositor's Bible Commentary*, the Greek word used in the Galatians passage, *historeō*, implies that Paul heard Peter's story, his eyewitness account of Jesus.
- Time in Tarsus (Acts 9:30, Galatians 1:21, Acts 11:25–26)—After a brief sojourn to Syria, Paul settled in Tarsus. More than a decade later, Barnabas took Paul to Antioch, which later became his base for his missionary journeys.

With what you know about Paul's life before salvation, his dramatic salvation, and his call to ministry, brainstorm a bit about his early years as a believer. What do you imagine God was doing in his life during his time in Arabia, Damascus, Jerusalem, and Tarsus?

God called, equipped, and gifted Paul for a unique purpose. Paul knew the same is true for every believer. He understood that our equipping and calling to ministry are works of God's grace in our lives. Encouragement to grow and challenges to serve fill his writings. As we explore some of these, ask God to encourage and challenge you!

Read Romans 12:4–8. Check any of the comments below that are true.

❑ Individual Christians have different work to do.

❑ God designed the Church in such a way that we cannot live out our faith on our own; we all need each other.

❑ God gives each Christian gifts of grace to equip us to carry out our unique work.

❑ We are free to choose whether or not we want to use our gifts in His service.

Now read 1 Corinthians 12:4–7 to add to our understanding of spiritual gifts. Briefly answer the following questions.

Does every believer get the same spiritual gift or gifts?

Is every believer called to the same ministry or service?

What is the source of our gifts?

What is the purpose of our gifts?

How does verse 7 define spiritual gifts?

The truths in these last two passages have helped, challenged, and encouraged me again and again. Over the years, I have struggled with jealousy. Jealousy over the way God is mightily using a fellow believer. Jealousy over a wonderful spiritual gift God has given someone else. Jealousy over the impact another is making for the kingdom of God. My pride and selfish ambition rise up and throw me off track. But God's Word convicts me and reminds me of what is true. All gifts are for His glory and the good of the church. He alone decides how to distribute His gifts of grace. My gifts are not for me but for others. These truths leave no room for jealousy, pride, or selfish ambition. Everything is by God's grace alone.

✎ Have you ever struggled with jealousy or wondered why God gifted you the way He has? How can absorbing the truths found in the last two passages help?

How has this week's lesson expanded your understanding of God's grace working in your life since salvation?

LIVING IT

I've been struggling recently with tendinitis in my right arm. Some days it even hurts to twist the lid off the toothpaste. On even worse days it hurts to lift the coffee cup. That's when I knew I had to do something quick! Ice, rest, and changing the position of my keyboard have helped.

Even this relatively small physical struggle reminds me I can't function at my physical peak unless all the parts of my body are well, strong, and doing their part. It's the same with Christ's body, the church. Unless every member of the body is functioning properly the church cannot optimally fulfill God's purposes. That includes me. That includes you. You cannot completely fulfill God's unique purpose for you without being a vital, serving, and maturing member of a local church body. The local church body cannot be everything God designed it to be without you.

God graciously calls every believer to a place of ministry and service. He gives us "gifts of grace" to equip us to obey that call. And all along the way, His grace teaches and challenges us to spiritual growth.

Have you given much thought to how those truths apply specifically to you? God has called you to a life of service and to a particular place of ministry. He has equipped you to obey. He challenges you to continued spiritual growth.

Read 1 Corinthians 12:7, 12–27, and answer the following questions.

Who receives spiritual gifts?

Why does the Spirit give spiritual gifts?

What percentage of members should use their gifts in order for the church to function as God intends?

Have you discovered your unique place of service and ministry within a local church and in His kingdom? Are you fulfilling the role God designed for you? If not, why? What changes can you make to step into His calling?

I want to interject a caution. Ministry and service can turn into mere "busy work" unless we continually pursue a deepening relationship with Jesus and purposefully strive to grow in our understanding and faith. In Paul's letter to his spiritual "son" Timothy, he reminded the younger man of the immeasurable value of spiritual growth.

☞ Read 1 Timothy 4:7–8, and answer the following questions.

What does the phrase "train yourself" imply about your role in your spiritual growth?

What value does commitment to godliness bring?

What are you currently doing to "train yourself"?

Do you need a different or more purposeful training program? If so, what changes will you make today?

GRACE APPLIED

Dove began a relationship with Jesus when she was just a young girl, but it took more than 25 years to discover God's unique purpose for her life. Dove accepted Jesus as her Savior when she was six. Her mother modeled a mature, devoted relationship with Jesus and Dove had a solid church, Christian friends, and opportunities to learn and grow. But like many young believers, Dove failed to keep Jesus first during college and her early years of marriage.

Then God began intervening to get Dove's attention. At the time, she loved her job as an office manager. The position required her to lead others in a variety of areas and juggle a wide range of responsibilities. She constantly gained new skills and experiences.

Dove particularly enjoyed the leadership aspects of her job. She felt gifted in this area and believed she found her niche. Great job, great family. Life was good; Dove was content.

Then several things happened that made her feel unsettled, as though God had something more for her to do. First, Dove's pastor began preaching a series on spiritual disciplines. God used the teaching to equip and encourage Dove to dig deeper in her relationship with Jesus.

Next, challenges and changes arose at work and in her family, and she found herself turning to Jesus even more. Then one Sunday morning, her pastor preached on the first chapter of Joshua. God seemed to amplify His Words. "Be strong and courageous, because you will lead these people to inherit the land . . . Be careful to obey . . . Keep this Book of the Law always on your lips; meditate on it day and night, so that you may be careful to do everything written in it" (Joshua 1:6–8).

God's Word hit home. "I felt convicted that though I had been a Christian for 25 –years, I had not really made His Word central in my life. Right there in my seat, God began to bring together earlier conversations and previous convictions to clarify a calling to full-time ministry." That morning Dove responded with obedience and went forward to tell the church.

Although Dove didn't yet have specific direction from God as to a place of ministry, she knew she would follow wherever He led. She immediately began taking seminary courses to prepare. Just six months later, her church asked Dove to be the children's ministry director at their second campus.

Looking back, Dove can see how God used her corporate job to prepare her for the ministry position. At the small second campus, Dove is responsible for a host of areas, not just the children. "God is using the skills He developed in me as an office manager for bigger, kingdom purposes. He also prepared me to lead others. That's what I get to do here. I get to lead others and help them grow to spiritual maturity. I get to help others find and follow God's purpose for them!"

In what ways did God prepare Dove before He clarified His call to vocational ministry?

How did Dove discover God's specific direction for her?

Although God does not call every believer to full-time vocational ministry, He does call each of us to specific areas of ministry and specific tasks. He has a unique purpose for every believer. Have you discovered yours? If so, describe it.

Some of you may be seeking God's unique purpose for you for the first time. Others may be discovering a redirection or refining of His call. What can you do to purposefully find and follow His leading? (Keep in mind that God wants you to know His will for you. He does not keep it hidden.)

PART TWO

GRACE
POURED THROUGH

*God calls believers to be
channels of His grace to others.*

Nicky Cruz was once the warlord of the notorious Brooklyn street gang, the Mau Maus. In the 1950s, the Mau Maus ruthlessly ruled the streets, even terrorizing the police. Caught in a cycle of violence, drugs, alcohol, and sex, Nicky was arrested countless times. In his autobiography, *Run Baby Run*, Cruz describes himself during this time of his life as a "mad dog."

Then in July 1958, a young preacher named David Wilkerson held a rally in the Mau Mau's turf. Nicky and some of his gang friends threatened to kill the preacher, but the story of Jesus' Crucifixion broke Nicky and the gospel message pierced his heart. Within a few weeks, Nicky gave his life to Christ at a rally at the St. Nicholas Arena.

Leaving his old life wasn't easy, but God graciously intervened, protected, and provided for Nicky in countless ways. For instance, God provided a way for Nicky to attend Bible college in California, and Nicky became a minister of the gospel that had transformed his life.

Immediately after graduation, Nicky began to extend the grace God had given him. He returned to New York to share Jesus with his old friends and others like them who were still on the streets. Nicky served as the director of Teen Challenge, a ministry to help troubled teenagers that was founded by David Wilkerson, the preacher pivotal to Cruz's conversion story. Nicky also later founded a ministry home in California.

Nicky got it—the depth of God's undeserved grace. He lives his life as a grateful response to the grace God so generously poured out on him. Paul got it, too. He had experienced God's grace in lavish abundance. Paul knew everything he had, everything he was, and everything he would be and accomplish depended solely on God's unbounded grace.

> *But whatever I am now, it is all because God poured out his special favor on me—and not without results. For I have worked harder than any of the other apostles; yet it was not I but God who was working through me by his grace.*
>
> —1 CORINTHIANS 15:10 NLT

Only by God's grace. Paul was nothing without it. He knew it and he never forgot it. God's grace motivated and colored everything Paul did and said. His life was a channel of God's free-flowing, unlimited grace, not merely a receptacle.

The same should be true for you and me. God calls us to be channels of His grace, not stagnant pools. When we truly understand the depth of His undeserved grace in our own lives, we would not dare withhold it from others. In his book *Putting a Face on Grace*, Richard Blackaby reminds us of God's call to be people that freely share God's grace with others.

> We are not called to just bathe in grace; we are called to shower it upon others. Grace has not been fully experienced until it is fully expressed to others. The deeper our understanding of grace, the more we see the necessity of making it the fabric of our Christian life.

LEARNING IT

Yes, Saul experienced God's grace without bounds, but he quickly learned that God's people aren't always as gracious. In this week's lesson, we will witness Saul's treatment in Jerusalem, explore his teaching on gracious words, and discover how we can express grace in everything we say and do.

First, let's try to grasp, even in a small way, what those early Christians felt about Saul and his claim to faith in Christ. Pretend for a moment you are a disciple of Christ in the first century in Jerusalem.

Imagine you were on the street the day Stephen was stoned. You saw that young, zealous Pharisee named Saul give consent to Stephen's death and encourage the crowd to throw the stones. You saw the murderous intent on his face. Over the next few years you heard many stories about Saul and his cruel, violent efforts to wipe out all the Christ followers. Then one day you heard he was back in Jerusalem wanting to join the fellowship of believers.

How do you think you would feel about Saul after he claimed to have a conversion experience? How would you have treated him when he came to Jerusalem?

Read Acts 9:26–30. Indicate the correct sequence of events from this passage by numbering the following statements from 1 to 5.

_____ Barnabas came alongside Saul and smoothed the way with the other believers in Jerusalem, convincing them of his conversion and fearless testimony.

_____ The Jerusalem believers learned of a plot to kill Saul so they sent him safely to Tarsus.

_____ Saul fled to Jerusalem to escape danger in Damascus.

_____ Saul became part of the Jerusalem fellowship and spoke boldly about Jesus.

_____ The believers in Jerusalem feared Saul and would not accept him because they didn't believe he had really been saved.

🕮 Now, consider Barnabas. He treated Saul differently. Read the following passages, and record what each teaches us about Barnabas or his treatment of Saul.

Acts 4:36–37

Acts 9:26–28

Acts 11:25–26

Acts 13:1–3

Why do you think Barnabas treated Saul differently than the other Jerusalem believers treated him?

Honestly, I would have probably been one who fearfully shunned Saul. Can't you identify? But that's our way, not God's way. Grace is God's mode of operation. So, God used Barnabas as His tool of grace in Saul's life. When the Jerusalem believers locked Saul out of their fellowship due to fear and suspicion, Barnabas was the key of grace that opened the way. When Barnabas needed help leading and discipling the believers in Antioch, he went to Tarsus and brought Saul back to minister alongside him. And when God's call came to take the gospel abroad, Barnabas was Saul's first missionary partner.

Reread Acts 9:26–28. These verses don't record Barnabas's actual words, just his actions and the results. But we can be sure his words both expressed grace and encouraged the apostles to act with grace. Based on what you know, write what you imagine Barnabas might have said to the apostles to open the door of acceptance for Saul.

Barnabas — encourager, advocate, and mentor — purposefully extended God's grace to the man who would write more about grace than any other biblical author. No doubt, God used the graciousness of Barnabas to help shape Saul into the man God desired. Grace heals and encourages, transforms and motivates. In *Putting a Face on Grace*, Blackaby describes this aspect of grace, "Grace looks at what people can become and seeks to help them reach their potential."

Grace did not see "Saul the persecutor." Grace saw "Saul, child of God, chosen minister of the gospel." God's grace, poured out through Barnabas, helped Saul reach his God-given potential.

TEACHING IT

In the early years of our marriage, Wayne and I moved to another city for his job. Our new house had a breakfast area, but we did not have a breakfast table. I really wanted a casual table for that area, an everyday place for us to eat as a family. It took a year or so to convince Wayne we needed one and then a while to find one we both liked and could afford. I was so proud of that table.

We only had the table a few months when my parents came all the way from Louisiana to visit us in Wyoming. The time came for dinner and we all gathered around the table to sit. Mom pulled out her chair and sat. As she scooted forward, a leg of the chair caught in the groove between two tiles. The leg snapped off, the chair tilted, and my mother hit the floor. Hard.

My immediate reaction was not words of grace. Oh, no. "You broke my chair!" is what came out of my mouth. Not, "Are you alright?" or, "Let me help you!" My mother looked so hurt. Not physically; the tumble wasn't too bad. But I terribly hurt her feelings. My words revealed that my first thought had been for the chair, not her.

Even words spoken without malice can wound.

Paul knew our words have the power to build up or tear down. God can use our speech to give grace to those who hear. I don't know about you, but this is a tough area for me. The tongue is hard to tame (James 3:7–8). Paul knew that, too. But Paul understood the unbounded nature of God's grace is more than sufficient to tame our tongue.

Read Ephesians 1:1–8 to get Paul's whole thought. Now look back at verses 6–8. List any words or phrases that help you understand the "unbounded" nature of God's grace.

Depending on your Bible translation, you found descriptive words and phrases like "freely given," "riches," "poured out," "abounded," and more. God pours out His grace on us freely, richly, and without bounds!

My favorite English word used in this passage to describe God's grace is found in verse 8 in the NIV. "In him we have redemption through his blood, the forgiveness of sins, in accordance with the riches of God's grace that he lavished on us" (vv. 7–8). There it is at the end. *Lavished.* God is not stingy with His grace! He lavishes it on His children.

According to *Mounce's Complete Expository Dictionary of Old and New Testament Words*, the Greek word translated as "lavish" in the NIV and "abounded" in the KJV means "to abound, be in abundance, overflow." Think about this: God doesn't give us just enough grace to get by. He doesn't even give us a "generous" amount. He gives us grace in such abundance we cannot hold it all. It overflows our ability to contain it. Praise God! What are we to do with this lavish, abundance of grace?

Have you ever squirted lotion into your hand from a tube, only to have far more plop out than you could ever work into your skin? If you're like me, after you've rubbed some into your hands—and elbows—you look for a friend or two with whom to share the abundance. Lotion for everyone!

Grace is like that lotion. More than we could possibly use ourselves. It is abundant, overflows our lives, and spills out all over. God has lavished us with His grace so we can freely and generously share it. Let's see what that looks like for our speech.

Read Ephesians 4:29 from your favorite translation and then from the KJV below:

> *Let no corrupt communication proceed out of your mouth,*
> *but that which is good to the use of edifying, that it may*
> *minister grace unto the hearers.*

Based on the KJV translation, what should be the primary result of every-thing we say?

The translation I use most often translates the Greek word, *chàris*, in Ephesians 4:29 as "benefit." Knowing that my speech should give "grace" to others gives me a deeper sense of responsibility and intent about what comes out of my mouth, rather than simply thinking it should "benefit" others.

Flip back to the "Teaching It" section of Week One and review the defini-tion of *chàris*. Then write a "purpose statement" for your speech. Include how your words should affect those who hear them.

Paul also uses three other words/phrases to describe what our words should and should not be—one negative and two positive. What are they?

1.

2.

3.

Depending on your translation, these three Greek words are trans-lated into various English words. Here are some facts from *Vine's Complete Expository Dictionary of Old and New Testament Words* that show possible English words and the Greek definitions for the three descriptive words in the order Paul wrote them.

1. *Sapros*: Corrupt, foul, dirty, unwholesome—"rotten, putrid, and unfit for use." It was used to refer to rotting fruit or vegetables.
2. *Agathos*: Helpful, good, beneficial—"Describes that which, being 'good' in its character or constitution, is beneficial in its effect."
3. *Oikodomé*: Edifying, build up, encouragement—"The act of building; this is used only figuratively in the [New Testament], in the sense of edification, the promotion of spiritual growth."

Corrupt speech is far more than curse words. Corrupt speech is graceless speech. Corrupt speech tears down, deflates. Picture a beach ball, fully inflated. Now imagine that ball is your spouse, your child, your co-worker, or your friend. Anytime you speak "corrupt" words, they deflate. Any words not wholesome or beneficial tear them down emotionally and spiritually. See the ball deflate? Little by little the air goes out. Sadly, I've seen my own words have that effect on other people.

Now picture that ball again, in desperate need of air before it can be used for its purpose. Like air blown into that limp beach ball, good and edifying words encourage and build up an individual, helping them reach their full potential in Christ. If we cooperate and allow God's grace to flow through us and out of our mouths, He can use our tongues as instruments of His grace. Our words will encourage, edify, build up, and *grace* those who hear them.

LIVING IT

I tend to open my mouth and allow words out before I consider their effect. But I don't think I'm alone. "Speech" seems to be one of the most difficult areas—if not, the most difficult—for many Christian women. Why is that?

A former pastor often said, "What's in the well comes up in the bucket." This phrase, which I've heard many times since, reflects a truth Jesus declared during a discourse with the Pharisees.

Read Matthew 12:33–37. What does Jesus' metaphor about trees and fruit teach us about our speech?

This passage has some interesting connections to what we've seen this week in Ephesians 1:8 and 4:29. First, "bad" or "corrupt" in verse 33 is the same word Paul used for "corrupt" or "unwholesome" speech in Ephesians 4:29 (*Vine's Complete Expository Dictionary of Old and New Testament Words*). Second, the Greek word translated as "overflow" or "abundance" in Matthew 12:34, is the noun form of the verb translated as "lavished" or "abounded" in Ephesians 1:8 (*Mounce's Complete Expository Dictionary of Old and New Testament Words*).

Our words directly reflect the condition and content of our hearts. Sometimes our own insecurities produce "ungracious" words. Sometimes hurt, unresolved anger, or fear is the culprit. And sometimes, the "overflow" of our hearts is greed, selfishness, pride, or defensiveness. We know the power of words, and unfortunately sometimes we use them as weapons.

I don't want to tear down and hurt others with my words. I want to encourage, build up, and help. What about you? Since our words begin in our hearts, that's the place we must start.

Take a few moments and reflect on some recent conversations you know did not "give grace" to the hearers. Ask God to show you what was in your heart. Record what He shows you below.

Now ask God to help you honestly evaluate the words you use, particularly with those closest to you. (That's often when all the "filters" fall away and our words most accurately reflect what's in our hearts.) Maybe you need to ask for forgiveness, commit to a "word overhaul," or seek God's help in one particular area or with one specific person. Record what God tells you.

God desires our hearts to be a conduit for the "overflow" of His grace. If we let Him, His grace can push out all the junk stored in our hearts. Here are a few things we can do to foster "gracious" overflow:

• Regularly reflect on the unbounded grace God lavishes on us.
• Remember that God will hold us accountable for every word spoken (Matthew 12:36).
• Constantly check our hearts for sinful attitudes and motivations and confess them.

- Ask God to heal old hurts, soothe anger, and humble pride.
- With God's grace flowing through us, our words can be tools of grace God uses to build up, encourage, and edify.

GRACE APPLIED

If there was ever a time Lori "deserved" to be yelled at by her 15-year-old son, Josh, this was it. First, she got caught up with her own stuff at home and was late leaving for driver's training. On top of that, Lori made a few wrong turns, running them half an hour late. When a teenaged boy is waiting to get behind the wheel of a car, 30 minutes feels like an eternity.

As they pulled into the lot, Lori glanced down and realized she had forgotten to fill the gas tank. Lori planned to leave the car for Josh to use for his driving practice. Already flustered and upset with herself, Lori meekly confessed this additional failing to her son. He quietly replied, "It's OK, Mom. There's enough gas for practice. We can fill it up on the way home."

Ready for this scene to end, Lori quickly told Josh goodbye and climbed into her friend's waiting car. "Thanks for coming," Lori greeted her. "I feel like you're coming to my rescue! Coffee today is my treat!" Then off they drove—with the keys Lori should have given to Josh in her coat pocket.

Josh assumed Lori left the car keys in the ignition. So later, when it was time to drive, he pulled on the driver's door handle only to be greeted by the wailing sound of the car alarm. To make the embarrassing situation worse, more than a dozen young drivers witnessed it. By the time he reached his mom on her cell phone and Lori returned with the keys, another hour had passed. An hour with Josh standing beside the car, horn honking and lights flashing.

Most teenagers in the same situation would have been angry. Many would have used harsh words. Lori began apologizing even as she climbed out of her friend's car, but Josh stopped her with a strained smile. No angry words. No teenage drama.

Later at home, Lori asked Josh how he had been able to deal with the situation with such grace. "Mom, everyone makes mistakes." Then with a sly grin he added, "But maybe we should leave a little earlier tomorrow." Josh realized Lori had been upset over the situation and didn't want to add to her angst. He knew harsh words would only hurt her more. Although Josh was frustrated, he made a conscious choice to react in a way that would help instead of hurt. He chose grace.

Josh chose to respond to his mother with words of grace. How would things have gone differently if he had chosen to respond with "corrupt" words?

Situations like this one happen every day among families and friends. Think about the last time you encountered one. Briefly describe it.

Did you and the others involved in the situation use words of grace or graceless words? How could the situation have turned out differently?

The next time you find yourself in the middle of a similar situation, what are some ways you can purposefully choose to help the situation?

"The Gift of the Magi," a classic short story written by O. Henry, was first published in 1905. Adapted for both film and stage, the story has been retold countless times. And now, even more than a century later, the story still captures our attention.

A young married couple, Jim and Della Young, live in a small apartment and barely earn enough to pay their bills. Although poor, they each own one thing they prize. Della's cherished possession is her thick mane of chestnut colored hair, which flows down past her knees. Jim's gold pocket watch is a family heirloom, which belonged to his father and his father's father before him. Jim always keeps the watch with him even though the leather strap that holds it is old and worn.

As Christmas draws near, each longs to give the other a special gift. Della scrimps and saves from her household money but manages to save just $1.87. Desperate to give her husband a gift that will adequately express her love, Della sells her beautiful hair for $20 on Christmas Eve. She scours the shops and finds the perfect gift—a platinum chain for Jim's watch.

Meanwhile, Jim also searches for the perfect token of love for Della. He knows Della longs for the expensive hair combs she had spotted in a shop window. Unable to pay for the tortoise shell hair combs with jeweled rims any other way, Jim sells his watch to purchase that one special gift for his beloved wife.

When Jim returns home on Christmas Eve they exchange the gifts and discover the true prize: each one willing to give up the possession they held most dear to demonstrate their love to the other.

Yes, the irony in the story makes for a bittersweet ending. But it's not the twist in the plot that makes this story a timeless favorite. No, the story endures because we all want to be loved like that. And we dare hope to love someone else like that—willing to submit our own desires and even needs to the other and put them first.

This is the heart of gracious relationships—loving others like God loves us and submitting ourselves to their needs. This week we'll take a closer look at two of Paul's relationships to see how he learned to let grace reign. Then we'll explore his teaching about relationships and seek to apply it all to our own lives.

LEARNING IT

We get a glimpse of Paul growing in grace through his relationship with the young John Mark. (Note: According to *Eerdmans Dictionary of the Bible*, John is derived from his Jewish name and Mark from his Roman name. Scripture refers to him variously as "John," "Mark," or "John Mark.") The Bible first introduces us to John Mark in Acts 12:12. The early believers gathered at his mother's house in Jerusalem to pray for Peter's release from prison.

John Mark and Barnabas were cousins (Colossians 4:10), which may be why Barnabas included John Mark on that first missionary journey with Saul. But something went wrong along the way and John Mark became a source of contention for Saul and Barnabas. Let's see how much of the situation we can piece together.

Read the following Scriptures, and note the facts you discover from each passage about John Mark and his relationship with Paul.

Acts 13:1–5

Acts 13:13

Acts 15:36–41

Colossians 4:10–11

2 Timothy 4:11

Philemon 1:24

Scripture doesn't tell us why John Mark left during the middle of the missionary journey or why it created such strong feelings in Paul. Although scholars suggest various things like homesickness and a disagreement over taking the gospel to the Gentiles, one strong possibility relates directly to Paul himself.

Reread Acts 13:13, and compare it with 13:2 and 13:7. What changes do you see in the way Scripture refers to the missionary team of Barnabas and Saul?

More than likely, Barnabas led the missionary team at the beginning. Scripture indicates this by the way Luke—the author of Acts—initially recorded their names as "Barnabas and Saul." Then two significant changes occurred. First, Luke began to refer to "Saul" as "Paul." (We will take a closer look at the significance of this change in our next lesson.) Second, "Barnabas and Saul" became "Paul and his companions" in verse 13. This change indicates a shift in leadership, according to the *Book of Acts: An Introduction and Commentary*. Barnabas stepped back and Paul stepped forward.

In what ways could this change have strained relationships among members of the missionary team?

Although we can't definitively determine the cause of the rift, we know it left Paul unwilling to include John Mark on the second missionary journey. And that caused a "sharp disagreement" with Barnabas. (Ah, even maturing Christians can struggle in their relationships.) Scripture doesn't give us the details, but we do learn that at some point, Paul gave John Mark a second chance. Grace had its way.

About ten years after the dispute with Barnabas over John Mark, Paul found himself in a situation that not only gave him the opportunity to treat someone with grace but also to encourage another to respond with grace.

A slave named Onesimus ran away from his owner Philemon. Onesimus then connected with Paul who was under house arrest in Rome. Paul shared the gospel with him and Onesimus became a Christian. In the first century, runaway slaves had no rights and no protection under the law. But in Christ all people are equal; there is no difference between slave and free (Colossians 3:11). How could Paul handle this situation with grace?

🕮 Read Philemon 1:8–21, and answer the following questions.

In what ways did Paul show grace to Onesimus?

In what ways did Paul show grace to Philemon?

How did Paul encourage Philemon to act with grace?

I don't think any of us would use Saul of Tarsus as an example of gracious behavior. And it seems that even Paul as a young believer still had a bit to learn about being a channel of God's grace. But grace certainly flowed through Paul in his relationships with the runaway slave Onesimus and his owner Philemon. Paul not only demonstrated grace, he also taught us about gracious relationships in his letters. Let's see what we can learn!

TEACHING IT

Last month on my birthday, my husband gave me a bag of my favorite chocolates—Lindor truffles. The luscious balls of decadent milk chocolate wrapped in shiny red foil belonged to me. So, the next day, as I was preparing for our home group Bible study, I hid the Lindors in the pantry and set out the everyday chocolate—some fun-sized Hershey bars. After all, I possessed a limited supply of the Lindor truffles. And I was absolutely not willing to share.

Unfortunately, sometimes we Christians act the same way with God's grace. We stingily hoard it for ourselves as if the supply will soon run dry. Either we forget the nature of God's grace or we need to expand our understanding. God calls us to be people of grace who relate to others with love, humility, and selflessness. But too often, pride and selfishness hinder our relationships.

How should we relate to others? What do relationships marked by grace look like? Paul elaborated on this topic in the Book of Ephesians. The first three chapters detail what God's grace accomplishes in our salvation. The last three chapters show us how to practically live a life of grace.

Read Ephesians 5:1–2 to discover the primary, divine characteristic that should define a believer's life. What is it?

The Greek word *agapé* describes God's love for us. It is love expressed in deliberate action. It seeks the welfare of others. It is not dependent on emotion, but is an act of the will. *Agapé* is based on the giver's character, not the worthiness of the receiver. *Agapé* is the distinguishing characteristic of gracious relationships.

How is the kind of love God commands us to have for each other different from the way the world loves?

The world's kind of love is a feeling and God's love is a choice. Feelings ebb and flow. Some days we will feel like showing love and other days we will not. But *agapé* is a firm decision to love someone else—not because we feel like it or because they deserve it—but because we are called to act in love. Just as God chose to act in love toward us even though we did not deserve it. His choice to love us was also the ultimate act of grace. "But God demonstrates his own love for us in this: While we were still sinners, Christ died for us" Romans 5:8.

Now let's discover another overarching characteristic that should mark our relationships. Read Ephesians 5:21, and write it out below. Circle the verb Paul uses as a command. Underline the reason we should obey that command.

The word *submit* has been misused, misunderstood, and abused. Let's start by digging into the dictionary definition for the Greek word *hupotasso*, which is translated as "submit" in English.

According to *Vine's Complete Expository Dictionary*, the verb *submit*—found in Ephesians 5:21, 22, and 24—is "primarily a military term, to rank under, to arrange." In general use, it means to put things in an orderly fashion under something else. In Ephesians 5, the word is in its passive form, which communicates the idea of *voluntarily* yielding to an established hierarchy.

Read Philippians 2:3–4 to shed light on God's command in Ephesians 5:21. Write a description of what it means to willingly submit yourself to another person.

Think about your various relationships in life. Give a practical example of what it might look like to "submit" to the following people:

Spouse

Children

Friend

Neighbor

Co-worker

Church member

Stranger

Like love, submission in relationships contradicts the way the world operates. The world tells us to make ourselves look good, to put ourselves first, to make sure our own needs are met, to save the best for ourselves. *To hide the Lindors.* But God tells us to use Jesus as our model. To act with humility. To seek the welfare of others. To meet their needs. To care about the interests of others. *To share the Lindors.*

Voluntary submission is an act of grace. This "yielding" requires humility and selflessness. The basis of this position is our love for Christ and our desire to please and serve Him. The outcome is the unity and growth of the church and provision for and spiritual growth of the individual. (See Philippians 2:1–2 and Ephesians 4:1–16.)

☞ "Love" and "submission" may feel a bit abstract. Let's get a more concrete picture of a gracious life in action by filling out the chart below. Read the passages in the left column and list any behavioral characteristic you spot in the correct column.

SCRIPTURE	GRACELESS BEHAVIOR	GRACE-FULL BEHAVIOR
Romans 12:9-18		
1 Corinthians 13:4-8		
Ephesians 4:1-3		
Ephesians 4:31-32		

Are you feeling a bit overwhelmed? Remember, God knows we cannot speak or act in grace on our own. It is only by His power working in us and His grace flowing through us that we can be channels of His grace. God supplies everything we need to live a godly, obedient—and yes, grace-full—life (2 Peter 1:3).

LIVING IT

I've experienced it several times—the miracle in the Starbucks drive-through line. That thrilling moment when you order your drink, pull around to the window, and the barista announces that the person in front of you paid for your coffee.

My first reaction is always "Wow! That's awesome!" Then almost as quickly I think, "Man, I should have ordered a venti!" (That means "extra large" in the language of Starbucks!)

My gratitude initially fosters a desire to buy the coffee for the person behind me. But before I pull out my wallet, I check out the vehicle behind me to make sure it's not a 12-passenger van carrying a high school basketball team. I mean, I want to pass along the blessing, but there are limits.

Sometimes we feel that way about sharing God's grace. We want to actively love others and submit to them out of reverence for Christ. But some people don't deserve it. And others can't do anything for me. Oh, wait . . . that's the point of grace. By definition, "grace" means being kind to those who don't deserve it. To give and do without any expectation that the other person will reciprocate. To show kindness to those who have hurt us and meet the needs of those who will never be able to help us in return.

Are we ever stingy or choosy with the kindness God has freely given us? As believers, we have an abundant supply of His grace. God has given us more than we need; yet sometimes we hoard it. We withhold it from those who desperately need it.

In this section, as we seek to apply God's truth to our own lives, we'll consider two categories of people we may encounter—those who have hurt us and those who do not have the capacity to respond to us with grace.

☞ Read 2 Corinthians 1:12–13. Although the believers in Corinth mistreated Paul, he always treated them with grace. Prayerfully consider the following questions.

Can you think of an instance in your life when someone extended grace to you when you had mistreated him or her?

Is there someone in your life now that is always difficult or that hurts you repeatedly?

If so, how have you related to them in the past?

What would be some practical, specific ways you could allow God to flow His grace through you to them?

Now let's consider how we relate to those who cannot "grace" us in return. Sadly, our sinful nature tends to give with expectation. We invite a family to dinner and expect them to one day invite us to their home. We take a meal to a sick friend, give a ride, or do a favor hoping they will do the same for us in our time of need. While that expectation of reciprocation may not be our primary motivation, it is often still there. Lurking in the back of our minds, qualifying our grace.

🤚 Think about your recent acts of service. List every motivation you can think of.

What if there was no room for expectation? What about those people who have no ability to invite, to give, help, or offer? How quick are we to extend grace to the orphan, the widow, the homeless, the invalid, the dying? Many of us find it easy to give money and goods, but what about our time and attention?

Jesus spent a lot of time around these kinds of people. He healed, He touched, He gave. The One "who came from the Father, full of grace and truth" (John 1:14) extended grace with no expectation of return. Jesus calls us, His followers, to treat others the same way.

🤚 Read Matthew 25:31–46, and answer the following questions.

What acts of grace does Jesus expect from His followers?

To what type of people should we extend grace?

What is the higher, spiritual impact of extending grace with no expectation of return?

There are many hungry and needy people in the world. In fact, the need can be so overwhelming we don't know where to begin. While we cannot meet all the needs, we can meet some. Many wonderful Christian organizations exist that work on a global scale, like World Vision, Compassion International, and Samaritan's Purse. You may not know where to start, but they do. Connect with a reputable organization, and donate your time or money.

What other organizations do you know of that make an impact around the world or in your community? How might you connect with them?

Now think a little closer to home. Who are the people right around you—neighbors, friends, family members, church members—who are needy? Make a list.

In what ways are you already extending grace with no expectation of return?

☞ Ask God to show you how you might show grace in other specific, practical ways. Write what He tells you below.

GRACE APPLIED

Julie is the primary caregiver for her mother-in-law. Kay's dementia makes this trying situation more difficult. As her cognitive function continues to diminish, Kay becomes more dependent and demanding. Julie keeps giving more. Kay can only receive.

Kay and Julie's relationship has always been superficial. Julie and her husband Scott tried to foster the relationship and often invited his mom to visit them. They even offered to fly her to their home 600 miles away. But Kay usually declined, preferring to spend vacations and holidays with Scott's brother. In many other ways as well, Kay showed her preference for Scott's brother and his family.

Then when Scott's father passed away about 14 years ago, things began to change. He left Kay in solid financial shape, so for about a decade she did fine living on her own. But Kay's relationship with Scott's brother, who lived in town, became strained, and she began to accept Scott and Julie's invitations.

During Kay's visits, Julie worked hard to meet her expectations. She cooked the meals Kay requested and took her shopping at all her favorite stores. Every visit left Julie exhausted, but Julie was learning how to extend grace to a woman who treated her with disinterest and selfishness.

About four years ago the family began to notice significant memory problems in Kay and discovered she was deep in debt. As Scott worked through the financial issues, Julie regularly made the long drive to Kay's to get the house in order. After months of sorting through massive piles, cleaning out, donating, and boxing up, Kay came to live with Julie and Scott.

Julie's life changed immediately and drastically. Kay doesn't drive, cook, or do laundry. Plus the dementia has intensified her demanding tendencies. Kay doesn't often ask Julie to do something, she tells her. Kay's activities always take priority over Julie's. Kay still shows preference for the other grandchildren. But Julie realizes God is working through this one-sided relationship to refine and transform her, to chisel away her pride, and to foster selflessness.

Julie knows she's in a battle that only God can win.

Julie shares of her story, "I struggle daily. Daily God tells me His grace is sufficient. Some days I live in that truth. Some days I don't. On the best days, I cheerfully minister mercy. On the worst days, I ignore acts of mercy I could perform. Most days, I show love in actions while asking God to help me love her more. I don't have the grace to give her within my sinful self. I realize that every loving act and kind word is actually God's grace flowing through me by the presence and power of the Holy Spirit. I have to ask for that grace every day. Sometimes I try to justify my selfishness. Other times I feel bitterness creep in. But God always reminds me of His great grace to me. He is faithful."

Reflect on the definition of grace we learned in Week One. How does Julie's relationship with Kay demonstrate true grace?

Does this life of grace come easy for Julie? If not, what makes it difficult at times?

Is there a relationship in your life that is totally or mostly one-sided? If so, how have you been doing with meeting the expectations?

WEEK 5
96

Based on what you've learned this week and seen demonstrated in Julie's story, in what practical ways can you allow God to use you as a channel for His grace?

One Tuesday morning years ago, I had a "traffic incident" on my way to lead a ladies' Bible study. I started the drive frustrated with myself because I left the house late. Then two stoplights from my destination, the driver of the only car in front of me sat through the green light without moving. While busily chatting with her passenger, she missed the opportunity to turn left. I "patiently" waited behind her for the next green light.

When the light changed to green again, she continued to chat, but failed to drive. So I hit my horn. And no, not a friendly, quick toot. It was a long, irritated blast. She slowly began to move and we both barely made it through the intersection before the light changed again.

As soon as I had the chance, I darted around her, tossing back one of those icy glares as I sped by. I approached the last light and got in the right lane to make my turn. I glanced in the rear view mirror. "Distracted Driver" was also in the turn lane. One block from church, a horrible possibility hit me. What if Distracted Driver was also headed to my church?

A community group also met in our church building on Tuesday mornings. She would see me go in and know I was one of those "Christian" women. I slowed to make the turn into the church parking lot. Another furtive glance in the rear view confirmed my fear. Distracted Driver was turning, too. I quickly scooted into the one remaining parking spot close to the doors and she made her way further down the lot. I ducked inside the building and into my classroom before she had time to get her seatbelt unfastened.

The Holy Spirit swiftly convicted me. Instead of extending grace, I acted with impatience and anger. My behavior negatively impacted the name of Jesus. Instead of sharing the grace of Christ that day, I was just another example of a graceless Christian.

God woos people to Himself with grace. Yet far too often our witness is anything but gracious. Sometimes our ungracious behavior reflects poorly on Jesus. Sometimes, our verbal witness lacks grace. And still other times our spiritual conversations simply fail to connect with the hearer.

The Apostle Paul dedicated his life to sharing the gospel of grace with the lost. And he did it with grace. He behaved and spoke in a way that connected with others and honored Jesus. This week we will learn about being a graceful witness from Paul's life and teaching and seek to apply the truths to our own lives.

LEARNING IT

Saul the Pharisee was a Jew through and through. "Circumcised on the eighth day, of the people of Israel, of the tribe of Benjamin, a Hebrew of Hebrews; in regard to the law, a Pharisee" (Philippians 3:5). Yet Paul, God's missionary to the Gentiles, was a Roman citizen. He spoke Greek fluently, and understood the culture. He knew both worlds.

In Week Three, we learned how God called and uniquely equipped Paul to be a minister of the gospel to the Gentiles. His upbringing, background, education, and life experiences allowed him to move easily between the cultures. Paul could identify with and relate to both Jew and Gentile. And he made the most of this advantage to take the gospel of the Jewish Messiah to the non-Jewish world.

🙠 Read the following passages, and identify actions Paul took to put himself or a member of his ministry team on common ground with and purposefully connect with a specific group of people.

Acts 13:1–9

Acts 16:1–3

Let's look closer at both passages. On their first missionary journey, God connected Barnabas and Saul with the highest Roman official on Cyprus, the proconsul Sergius Paulus. This Gentile leader "wanted to hear the word of God" (Acts 13:7). Clearly the Holy Spirit was working! When God miraculously overcame the opposition of an evil sorcerer to validate the gospel message, the amazed proconsul believed!

In the midst of reading this exciting encounter, let's not miss an important fact. In verse 9, Luke records, "Then Saul, who was also called Paul." From this point forward, Luke only refers to the apostle as "Paul." This shift does not reflect a name change, as has often been said, but rather a conscious decision on Paul's part to better fit in with the Roman environment.

According to the *Book of Acts: An Introduction and Commentary*, since Paul was a Roman citizen, he would have been given three names at birth. The third was Paul's Latin name, *Paullus*. In his book *The Ministry and Message of Paul*, Richard N. Longenecker describes the significance of this event:

Paul, whose call was to the Gentiles, undoubtedly saw
in this incident at Paphos something more of what a
mission to Gentiles logically involved. At this point in
the record, significantly, he begins to be called by his
Roman name, Paul, rather than his Jewish name, Saul
(Acts 13:9); for from this point on he is prepared to
meet a Gentile of the empire as himself a member of
that empire.

Paul purposefully made an accommodation to better fit in a predominately Roman environment. "Saul the Pharisee" became "Paul,
citizen of Rome."

☞ List all the benefits you can think of for Paul's ministry to the Gentiles
that would come from Paul using his Latin name.

Using his Latin name is just one example of the way Paul purposefully worked to clear away any hindrances to the gospel message.
Near the beginning of his second missionary journey, Paul met
Timothy, a young believer with a Jewish-Christian mother and a
Greek father. Paul wanted to add Timothy to the missionary team,
so he had him circumcised. Some think this action directly con-
flicts with Paul's solid stand against forced circumcision of Gentile
believers. But let's walk through this together.

Some legalistic Jewish Christians tried to force Gentile believers
to be circumcised. They wrongly "taught" that they had to observe
this part of the Jewish law to be saved. Several times in Paul's letters
he firmly denounced this false teaching.

Read Galatians 3:1–5 and 5:1–6. Put Paul's teaching regarding circumcision for Gentile believers into your own words.

Now read Acts 17:1–4 and 17:10–15. Considering Paul's usual custom when he entered a new city and Timothy's role in the ministry, why would Timothy's circumcision be important?

In what ways was circumcision for Timothy different than circumcision for the average Gentile believer?

When Paul met him, Timothy was an uncircumcised believer with a Jewish mother. Paul wanted to use him in ministry to the Jews, but Timothy's uncircumcised state was an obstacle. In *The IVP Bible Background Commentary*, author Craig S. Keener explains, "Under Jewish law at least as early as the second century, a person was presumed Jewish if his or her mother were Jewish; but even if that ruling was in effect in Paul's day, Timothy would not have been accepted as fully Jewish, because he had not been circumcised. . . . Paul makes him a full Jew for the sake of his witness to the Jewish community." Timothy's circumcision had no effect on his salvation, but it did open the door of ministry to the Jews so the gospel message could be heard.

Throughout his ministry Paul not only purposefully worked to remove roadblocks to the gospel, he also intentionally sought ways to build bridges and open doors to conversation. When God provided the opportunities, Paul always proceeded with grace. Let's look at two examples.

Read Acts 17:16–34, paying particular attention to Paul's conversation with the philosophers at the Areopagus. List any characteristics and methods you find in Paul's spiritual conversation and gospel presentation that built bridges and opened doors. For instance, did Paul use "Christian phrases" or terms they would understand? Did he belittle their way of life or did he seek to find a connecting point?

Read Acts 26:1–32. List any gracious characteristics and bridge-building methods you find here.

Most of us probably won't be given the opportunity to talk to Greek philosophers about Jesus on a hilltop in Athens or share our testimony with a king. However, we can employ Paul's gracious speech and respectful demeanor. Here are some things I noticed in these two passages:

• Paul paid attention to and used his surroundings.
• Paul used their style of conversation; he used general sentiments and words they would have known and accepted.
• Paul found something about which to commend them.
• Paul in no way compromised the gospel message, but he utilized their cultural ideas as a springboard to introduce spiritual truth.
• Paul stressed the need for repentance but was respectful and polite.
• Paul did not demean or insult their culture or customs.

TEACHING IT

In the late 1990s my husband's company moved us to Alberta, Canada. We lived outside of Calgary for six years and loved it. Although the differences aren't drastic between the southern United States and western Canada, we did make some adjustments in order to function, connect, and be understood.

For instance, we quickly learned that Canadians always take off their shoes when they enter someone's home. Whether there is snow on the ground or not, it's the polite thing to do. We also altered our language a bit. Albertans primarily speak English, but Canada has two official languages—English and French. In fact, many French words are commonly used by English-speaking Canadians. One example is *serviette* or "napkin" for you Americans. I adapted and set my dinner table with silverware and *serviettes*. But not all visitors to Canada adapt so quickly.

One summer I went with the youth from our church to northern Alberta to roof houses with World Changers. A few of our church's teens and I were assigned to a team with youth from a church in the States. At lunch one day, a Canadian teen asked an American teen to please pass her a *serviette*. The American teen didn't understand, so I explained. The American rudely rolled her eyes and scoffed, "Well, why don't you just call it a napkin then!" My shy Canadian girl quietly shrank back.

I quickly reminded the rude American teenager that she was a guest in Canada and should kindly call the square of paper what the Canadians call it.

Sadly, we Christians sometimes behave like the rude American teen. Rather than conforming to the customs of the culture we desire to impact with the gospel, we attempt to mold it to our own. I am not by any means suggesting we behave or speak in a way contrary to a godly lifestyle or that dishonors the name of Christ. But there are countless other ways we can connect to people who are different from us.

Paul purposefully worked to fit into the culture where he ministered. He sought to build bridges to earn trust and gain opportunity to share the gospel.

Read Acts 20:24. What was Paul's primary goal for his life?

Paul longed to fulfill God's calling on his life by "testifying to the good news of God's grace." He testified with both his life and his words. He constantly laid down his life to share the message of grace. Whatever it took. Wherever he had to go.

We saw Paul in action in the previous section. Now let's explore Paul's teaching on what a gracious witness should look like, in both our behavior and our speech.

🖙 Read 1 Corinthians 9:19–23. Describe in your own words the measures Paul willingly took to win the lost to Christ.

🖙 What exceptions or limits did Paul set? (See verse 21.) What does that look like for us today?

Paul set aside his own preferences, comforts, rights, and desires in order to build relationships and make opportunities to share Christ. "Christ's law" was his one qualifier. Paul willingly adopted the practices of those he sought to win unless they contradicted God's holy standards for His people. Observe Jewish ceremonial law to win the Jew? Sure! Eat a non-kosher meal in a Gentile home? Absolutely. Abstain from any food or drink that might prick the conscience of an immature believer? Yes, indeed.

In his commentary on 1 Corinthians, Leon Morris clarifies Paul's limit in "becoming all things."

> He sums it all up with *I have become all things to all men.* This does not, of course, mean that his conduct was unprincipled. On occasion his principles led him to follow courses of action in the teeth of strong opposition. But where no principle was at stake he was prepared to go to extreme lengths to meet people. Personal considerations are totally submerged in the great aim of by all means saving some.

Paul gladly laid down freedoms, rights, preferences, and desires if it meant he might bring someone to Jesus. His ministry of the gospel demonstrates grace—an intentional choice to, "Submit to one another out of reverence for Christ" (Ephesians 5:21).

Even imprisonment did not squelch Paul's desire to spread the gospel. In his letter from a Roman prison to the Colossian believers, he expressed his continued desire to spread the good news of Jesus.

Read Colossians 4:2–6. List the ways Paul asked the believers to pray for him.

Now list any instructions and guidelines Paul gives the believers regarding sharing their faith in Christ.

☞ What does it look like practically to "be wise in the way you act toward outsiders?" Read the following passages, and list any characteristics or actions that help us understand how believers should behave out in the world.

Ephesians 5:8–11

1 Thessalonians 4:11–12

1 Timothy 3:7

Titus 3:1–2

1 Peter 2:11–12

In *The Expositor's Bible Commentary*, Curtis Vaughan helps us understand Paul's command in Colossians 4:5.

> Paul's words imply that believers are to be cautious and tactful so as to avoid needlessly antagonizing or alien-ating their pagan neighbors. In a positive sense, they also imply that believers should conduct themselves so that the way they live will attract, impress, and convict non-Christians and give the pagan community a favor-able impression of the gospel.

All of a believer's conduct and behavior should honor Christ and positively impact "outsiders." But that's not the end game. People cannot respond to the gospel message unless they hear it. Our lifestyle should open the door to opportunities to verbally share the gospel.

Reread Colossians 4:6 and compare it to 1 Peter 3:15. List any adjectives and phrases that describe the correct kind of conversation with those who don't know Jesus.

The world needs the truth of the gospel delivered with grace. Unfortunately, believers sometimes compromise the truth of the gospel in an attempt to make it more palatable. Other times, we may boldly declare the uncompromising truth in a manner that repels. People won't respond to a dogmatic diatribe of right and wrong. We need both grace and truth. May our spiritual conversations always be "full of grace" (Colossians 4:6) and characterized by "gentleness and respect" (1 Peter 3:15).

LIVING IT

I have been on numerous short-term missions trips, but the greatest culture change I have experienced was in Bangladesh. Since the country is predominately Muslim, the role and dress of women is very different from the West. So we wore the *salwar kameez*, characterized by long tunic tops reaching almost to the knees, and an *orna*, a long scarf worn draped around the shoulders to cover the chest. We also studied the culture and practiced traditional Muslim greetings. When we met someone on the street we said, *assalam waleykum* (peace be with you). And if someone greeted us first we replied, *waleykum assalam* (and with you). We willingly adapted to the culture as best we could to not offend the people. Our efforts also showed we respected them and desired to make a connection.

↳ The culture differences between Bangladesh and America are glaring. However, there are also differences between you and your co-worker, family member, or neighbor who doesn't know Jesus. Note some of these differences and jot down ideas about how you can bridge that gap.

↳ Now think about how you can establish connecting points for building relationships. For instance, maybe your neighbor jogs every day and once asked you to join her. Or maybe your lost family member knits or your co-worker loves foreign films. Prayerfully consider possible connecting points and write down at least three actions you can take.

Reread Colossians 4:2–6. What specific changes can you make in your behavior or speech to be a more gracious witness?

Now write a prayer asking God to help you "be all things to all people," build connecting points, and graciously take advantage of every opportunity to share Jesus.

GRACE APPLIED

About four months ago, our friend Lee lost her husband after a long battle with cancer. They frequently traveled together, so Lee thought a long cruise might be restful and helpful while she sought to find her new normal. Lee chose a 30-day cruise that departed from Dubai then visited India, Seychelles, Kenya, and Mozambique on its way to Cape Town, South Africa.

Although she relished the time alone, Lee also purposefully sought to meet and build connections with the cruise staff and other passengers on the ship. God used Lee's willingness to connect as an opportunity to share God's truth with others.

During a luncheon one day for solo travelers, one gentleman told the group he was trying to figure out his next steps in life, to determine his purpose. So, Lee told the group about the biblical principles from Rick Warren's book *Purpose Driven Life*. Lee had sown seeds of truth.

Amazingly, God presented a similar opportunity at lunch the next day when Lee shared a table with a woman named Robyn in the crowded dining room. They chatted while they waited for their food. Robyn was reading a book she hoped would show her how to "increase her happiness." Once again, Lee recognized and took the God-given opportunity to share biblical truth about the meaning and purpose of life.

Lee's next "divine appointment" was with the woman staying in the cabin next door. Renee lost both of her parents in the previous three months. Still reeling with grief, she was reassessing her life after four years of caring for her parents full-time. She had actually thought about jumping overboard. "No one would know about my being gone for a long time," she sadly told Lee.

The door was open for Lee to talk about her own recent loss and how God had been meeting every need. As their spiritual conversation continued, Lee had the opportunity to talk specifically about a saving relationship with Jesus.

Lee did not see immediate results from any of these interactions, but she didn't need to. She boldly stepped out in obedience and shared God's truth through gracious conversation. The results are solely God's territory.

WEEK 6

111

In what ways did Lee seek to be "all things to all people" while on the cruise?

How did she seize the opportunities God presented to share?

Think back on some of your recent conversations and encounters. Did you miss any opportunities that you now see God provided? If so, how could you have handled them differently?

PART THREE

GRACE OVERFLOWING

*God's lavish grace floods our
lives during times of trial.*

WEEK SEVEN: WORK OF GRACE
GRACE NOTE: GOD GRACIOUSLY USES TRIALS FOR GOOD IN
THE LIVES OF HIS CHILDREN.

For our 30th anniversary, Wayne and I traveled to the island of St. John in the US Virgin Islands. We hiked and snorkeled and relaxed on the beach. It was glorious!

But one particular hike was more challenging than expected. The Ram Head Trail switches back and forth up a saddle back hill to the high, southern-most point of the island. Our tour book described it as a "steep, narrow, and slippery path, which can be tricky."

Since Wayne and I have done a lot of hiking, we felt confident we could manage this trail without a problem. We had plenty of water, snacks, and sunscreen. We both thought we had sturdy hiking boots.

That last sentence needs a bit of explanation. It had been quite a few years since I'd gone hiking so my boots had been sitting unused in the closet. Wayne encouraged me to buy some new ones, but since the boots I already had still fit and felt great, I insisted they were fine.

Halfway through the hike, my right boot began to feel strange. Upon examination, I discovered the sole had come loose from the boot at the heel, flopping against the ground with every step.

Wayne used a small elastic cord from his backpack to keep the sole tight against my heel. It worked for a while. Then the front of the sole released its grip on the toe of my boot.

Wayne found a piece of thin nylon rope right on the trial. We fastened that around my toe and started back up the trial. Although the sole slipped around a bit, it allowed me to walk without much trouble.

Then about 30 yards from the summit, the sole on the other boot came completely off. I picked it up and carried it the rest of the way to the top. With only a thin layer of fabric between the sole of my foot and the rocky trail, those last few yards were painful.

When I arrived, I plopped down on a large rock. How I was going to get back down the trail?

"Wish I hadn't left my sport sandals in the jeep," I complained out loud.

"I've got mine," Wayne offered. "Do you think you could wear them?"

Of course they didn't fit my *feet*, but they did fit nicely over what was left of my *boots*. I snugly tightened the Velcro straps and down the trail we went. The soles provided the grip I needed on the rocky path. And they stayed put! Wayne's sandals protected my feet and got me safely to the bottom.

Sometimes our lives are like that trail. The going gets steep and things start falling apart. We may even wonder how we'll go on. In those times of struggle, God wraps His strength around our weakness. He graciously protects our tender places. When we cannot go on, He carries us. His strength. His protection. His love and grace.

Paul repeatedly experienced trials, persecutions, and difficulties as he sought to fulfill God's calling. But he also abundantly received God's grace. The greater the trial, the greater the grace. Lavishly poured out.

In this third part of our study, we'll discover how God's grace overflows in our lives in times of difficulty. We'll rejoice in the truth that God's grace is available for every day and any day! In this week's lesson, we will lay a solid biblical foundation about the nature of trials. We will witness some of Paul's trials and discover how he viewed them through the lens of God's grace. We will also explore his teaching about how God uses trials in the lives of believers.

LEARNING IT

Although you've probably heard and read about many of Paul's trials, pulling the bulk of them together for a comprehensive look adds a dimension to his struggles we might miss otherwise. The sheer weight of his struggles highlights the depth of God's grace and strength in Paul's life.

Read the following Scripture passages and fill out the table. Skim the verses before and after each passage for additional information and context.

SCRIPTURE	LOCATION	NATURE OF TRIAL	SOURCE OF TRIAL	OUTCOME
Acts 9:22–25				
Acts 14:19–20				
Acts 16:19–24				
Acts 17:13–15				
Acts 18:12				
Act 21:27–36				
Acts 23:12–16				
Acts 24:27				
Acts 27:13–44				

I don't know about you, but if I faced even a portion of what Paul experienced I would have given God my resignation and headed home to Tarsus. But that reaction leaves no room for grace. Paul did not endure these trials by his own strength and determination. No, Paul kept pushing forward only because of God's grace, strength, and power working in his life.

If the chart above doesn't convince us of the enormity of God's miraculous intervention in Paul's circumstances consider this: Luke's record in Acts is just a sampling of the trials and struggles Paul faced. Paul describes and alludes to others in his letters. We won't look at them all, but we will venture into 2 Corinthians.

Paul established the church in Corinth during his second missionary journey. He was the Corinthians' spiritual father. But opponents were working to undermine Paul's authority over the church and his standing as an apostle. These opponents bragged about their "accomplishments" the same way the "world" does (2 Corinthians 11:18). So Paul "boasted" about his sufferings to show God's strength working in his weakness (2 Corinthians 11:30). His goal was to reveal the motives of his opponents and remind the Corinthian believers of his dedication to the gospel and of his love for them.

Read 2 Corinthians 11:22–33. Compare Paul's list of trials and struggles to your chart. List any additional incidents.

What do you think your own attitude about and response to similar circumstances would be?

Through all his hardships, Paul not only experienced the grace of God's strength and sustenance, but he also recognized that God worked through the trials to carry out His purposes and used them to grow Paul into the man God desired him to be. Let's look at two passages to discover what Paul learned.

🖝 Read 2 Corinthians 1:8–11, and answer the following questions.

List any words or phrases Paul used to describe the seriousness of his situation.

According to Paul in verse 9, why did God allow this to happen?

How did this act of deliverance impact Paul's attitude about future trials?

How does this situation demonstrate God's grace?

Scholars aren't sure what event Paul refers to in these verses, but it doesn't really matter. The important thing is God's miraculous intervention in a desperate situation—a situation so dire Paul believed he and his companions might die. He saw no way out of the life-threatening situation. Yet when all human hope was lost, God delivered them by His grace through the prayers of the believers.

Paul, a strong, well-educated leader with an enviable pedigree, was probably prone to pride and self-sufficiency. In fact, all of us have a sinful tendency to rely on ourselves, to accomplish things with our own strength and power. And while many of us are indeed strong and capable, our ability pales to God's. God longs for us to depend on Him, to realize our independence is only an illusion, and to allow Him to do what only He can do in and through our lives.

🐾 Read 2 Corinthians 12:1–10, and answer the following questions.

Describe Paul's experience.

What sinful attitude could easily develop after such a revelation?

What did God do to keep Paul's pride in check?

How did God answer Paul's prayer to remove the "thorn"?

God gave Paul a glimpse of heaven (2 Corinthians 12:1–4) during his early years as a believer, perhaps during his time of spiritual retreat in Arabia (Galatians 1:17). Paul didn't know if he had been physically transported or was there in spirit. But he saw and heard "inexpressible things." Pride would be the natural sinful response to an experience like this, but pride and conceit have no place in a servant of God. Therefore, God allowed something into Paul's life to foster humility—a "thorn of the flesh."

Paul's "thorn" is one of the biggest unknowns in Scripture. Over the centuries scholars have tossed out myriad suggestions such as a speech impediment, an eye problem, a recurrent malady like malaria, chronic Jewish persecution, and even some persistent temptation. But not enough evidence exists to come to a conclusion. So, we are left with an ambiguous "thorn" to which all of us can easily relate.

Like Paul, most of us have circumstances, troubles, or difficulties God has not eliminated from our lives. Though we repeatedly plead with Him to remove it, the pain remains. On some days, "My grace is sufficient," just doesn't feel sufficient. If we aren't careful we can begin to doubt God's power or His love for us.

Charles Swindoll addresses this topic in his book *Paul: A Man of Grace and Grit*:

> It is not always God's will that you be healed. It is not always the Father's plan to relieve the pressure. Our happiness is not God's chief aim. He doesn't have a wonderful (meaning "comfortable") plan for everybody's life—not from a human perspective. . . . As with Saul, His answer is not what we prayed and hoped for. But, remembering that He is forming us more and more into the image of His Son, it helps us understand His answer is based on His long-range plan, not our

immediate relief. Thankfully, in the midst of that suffering, He gently whispers, "My grace is sufficient for you."

TEACHING IT

God cares about every aspect of your life. He knows your every need and He cares deeply about each one. However, as much as He cares about your physical needs and condition, He cares even more about your spiritual condition. His first desire and primary purpose is to transform you into the image of Christ (Romans 8:29). The spiritual and eternal take priority over the physical and temporary. But how does God do the work?

Let's consider a physical analogy. If we want to strengthen our muscles we must add stress. When we lift a heavier load than our muscles have lifted before, a physical process begins to adapt the needed muscles to the new load. Without stress, our muscles are content with their current size and strength. Add stress, and our muscles begin to change to meet the need.

Our spiritual strength and character are similar. The difficulties of life stress our faith. Trials give our faith a workout like heavy loads work our muscles. As we faithfully endure, we grow spiritually stronger. Without difficulty, our faith tends to stagnate. Do you want stronger faith? You need stress.

What have you been taught about the nature of hardships in a believer's life?

Read John 16:33. Check any of the following statements that are true.
- ❏ We can experience peace in Jesus no matter our circumstances.
- ❏ Believers will face trouble in this world.

❑ Believers will not have to endure trials, difficulties, or hardship.
❑ Jesus is greater than any circumstance we will face.

We absolutely will face trials and difficulties in this life. Jesus not only taught it, He also experienced it. So did our friend Paul. But Paul also understood God's purpose for trials in believers' lives.

Read Romans 5:1–5. Based on this passage, answer the following questions with a "yes" or "no."

_____ Because of our relationship with Jesus, we live in a state of grace.
_____ We can rejoice over the results produced by the trials in our lives.
_____ The transforming work of trials is a process, not a quick work.
_____ Read James 1:2–4 and 1 Peter 1:6–7, compare these passages to Romans 5:1–5, and record anything new you learn about trials in a believer's life.

Jesus, Paul, Peter, and James agree. Everyone *will* experience difficulties, hardships, and temptations. Sometimes we are tempted by Satan or by our own sinful flesh. Sometimes God allows us to endure a time of testing to prove and strengthen our faith. And still other times we experience afflictions and burdens that are by-products of this fallen world.

But here's the good news for believers: Our gracious God never wastes a trial He permits to enter our lives. If we cooperate, He will use every difficulty, heartache, and hardship for our good and His glory.

Does what you've learned in this lesson conflict with what you have been taught to believe about trials in a Christian's life? If so, in what ways?

Before we consider what all this means to us personally, let's review what we've discovered in this lesson about the purpose of trials in a believer's life:

- God uses trials to break our independence and foster our dependence on Him.
- God uses trials to purify our faith and develop our moral character.
- God uses trials to test, prove, and strengthen our faith in Him.
- God uses trials to prepare us for His purposes.
- God works through trials to prove Himself powerful, faithful, and reliable.

Trials work our faith. Like using our muscles to become stronger and to carry heavier loads, the trials of life give our faith a workout. God will use them to grow and develop our faith so we will be spiritually mature, not lacking anything!

LIVING IT

Years ago, I realized that my friends with the strongest and most unshakeable faiths had faced many trials and difficulties. A friend with breast cancer. A friend who lost her mother. A friend whose husband couldn't find a job.

I noticed that not only was my life easy in comparison but also that my faith had grown stagnant. I continued to study God's Word and acquire more knowledge, but I knew there was much more. I began to pray that God would refine and strengthen my faith. And He answered.

Many difficulties began to pop up. Our house flooded. My mother-in-law was killed in a car accident. My husband's company transferred us to another city. All these things happened in the same few months. I had to cling to God, trust Him, and follow closely. The refining process had begun.

God is definitely not finished with me yet. I know more difficulties lie ahead. Honestly, I wish God had chosen to work another way. But I will choose to trust His infinite wisdom and submit to His refining process. I don't know about you, but I don't want to waste any trial or difficulty!

How would you describe your life right now? Check the statement below that most closely describes your life:

❑ My life is easy and trouble-free.
❑ I have a few small troubles, but they are all manageable.
❑ I have one or two big issues in my life weighing on my heart and mind.
❑ I am overwhelmed with hardship and don't know how I can go on.

☞ What have you learned in this week's lesson that applies to your life situation right now?

Where are you in the refining process? Are you willing and ready to allow God to use trials in your life for His purposes?

Trials work our faith. God uses them to refine us spiritually, to rid our hearts and minds of sinful attitudes and motivations. And as Paul discovered in the province of Asia, God uses struggles and difficulties to teach us to lean and depend on Him. As He proves Himself powerful, faithful, and reliable, our faith in Him grows and strengthens.

Are you convinced yet that trials are a work of God's grace in a believer's life? If not, maybe one more benefit will help you trust

God to work in and through every situation you face. We have yet to touch on it, but Paul knew it well.

🕮 Read Philippians 3:7–11, and answer the following questions.

Describe Paul's attitude regarding the comforts and treasures of this life.

What did Paul value most?

What blessings did Paul gain from suffering?

In this passage, "suffering" refers specifically to enduring persecution for the sake of Christ. While the intimacy with Christ that results from persecution is unique, every believer develops a deeper relationship with Jesus as we cling to Him during times of trials.

As we close this week's lesson, ask yourself how your attitude compares to Paul's. Do you welcome the work of grace God wants to do in your life through trials? Do you long to grow in your relationship with Jesus?

Wherever you are today, express your heart to God by writing your thoughts in a prayer below.

GRACE APPLIED

Three years ago, Donna had a busy life working full-time and raising three active children. Then she began experiencing chronic fatigue, dangerously low iron and blood pressure, vomiting, and fainting. Eating produced extreme abdominal pain. As Donna's health continued to deteriorate, she had to stop driving and quit the job she loved. She could no longer consume anything by mouth and had to get fluids and medication by IV. Donna, once a dedicated special education teacher and involved mom, had to depend totally on the care of her family.

Donna experienced months of hospitals, tests, procedures, and even a nursing home. She craved food but couldn't eat. Her weight dropped to 92 pounds. She was so weak, she couldn't get out of bed on her own. Family members took turns coming into town to be with her and help with the family.

Donna's physical battle was also a spiritual one. She was angry with God. Her joy in her relationship with Him was gone. "I couldn't fight for myself. I felt defeated. But then God, in all of His infinite power, abundant love, and unending grace, met me when I needed Him most. I felt His grace wash over me and I knew with Him I could handle whatever lay ahead. Prayer became food for me."

God regularly showed up in unexpected ways—a midnight text from a praying friend, encouragement from a Christian hospital roommate, words of wisdom from a brother-in-law. The physical battle continued, but Donna learned to depend on God's sustenance.

Finally, Donna received a double diagnosis—gastroparesis and sphincter of Oddi dysfunction. Gastroparesis is a chronic and incurable condition that prevents the stomach from emptying properly. And when the sphincter of Oddi doesn't work properly, digestive juices back up and cause severe abdominal pain. The surgery to correct it is high risk, but if left untreated it can be fatal.

God did not remove Donna's physical challenges, but He did work through a long series of treatments, a God-fearing surgeon, and gifted, caring medical personnel to give Donna a new normal. Today, Donna gets 90 percent of her nutrition pumped into her small intestine through a permanent jejunal tube, but she can also enjoy a few healthy foods in small quantities. She is back to work and vitally involved with her family and church.

Through this long and continuing journey, God has deepened Donna's relationship with Him and abundantly restored her joy. He gave her a testimony to His grace and faithfulness through a ministry to women suffering with similar health problems.

Donna acknowledges her life is a miraculous work of God's grace. She constantly leans on God, and His grace is sufficient for her. His power is constantly revealed in her weakness.

In what ways does Donna's life compare to Paul's "thorn in the flesh"?

How did God demonstrate His grace through Donna's struggles? How did God prove Himself strong through Donna's weakness?

Do you have a "thorn"? If so, what is it?

List ways God might use this thorn to work in your life and demonstrate His grace.

Week Eight: Power of Grace

Grace Note: In the midst of our trials God sustains us with His grace.

I woke in the middle of the night and the rawness of it all washed over me again. Our family faced a serious situation. I tried to fix it, but it seemed hopeless. I knew sleep would not come easily. I had no words left for prayer. I was prayed out.

Anxiety welled up and I reached for God. The Holy Spirit began to bring Scriptures to mind, so I began to pray them. Soon peace started to push out the anxiety until it was gone. Somewhere in the first chapter of 1 Peter, I drifted off to sleep.

At the time I was away from home staying with my oldest daughter. My grandson was just a few days old and I was helping out. The next morning, Kelley reported on how Micah slept the night before. Then almost as an afterthought she added, "The second time I came back to bed, Jeremy asked me to pray with him. He felt strongly we should pray for you right then."

"What time was that?" I asked.

"It was about 3:15 . . . 3:20," Kelley replied.

That was the same time I lay awake in bed with anxiety threatening to take over. I know because I had looked at my phone. God did not fix the situation like I'd hoped, but He was not idle. He saw my need and He cared. He poured out His grace through the heart of my son-in-law and gave me the peace and strength to keep going.

Sometimes God intervenes in our trials in physical ways. He heals. He frees. He delivers. But He does not always. God often works in far more miraculous ways. He pours out His grace to cover our soul needs.

God physically delivered Paul many times, like the release from prison shackles in Philippi. But it wasn't those physical rescues Paul marveled over. No, Paul preached passionately about the lavish, unbounded grace God poured out to sustain him in the midst of his trials.

As we learned last week, sometimes God allows struggles and difficulties to remain in our lives because He is using them to work out His spiritual and eternal purposes. He works in and through our trials to spiritually conform us to the image of Christ and to refine our faith and character.

In this week's lesson we will discover some of the ways God extends His grace in the midst of trials to comfort, encourage, and strengthen us while His "soul work" is being accomplished. We will also touch on ways God meets our physical needs even when He doesn't change the circumstances.

LEARNING IT

God's grace sustained Paul through a particularly difficult season of his life. As Paul neared the end of his third missionary journey, the Holy Spirit compelled him to go to Jerusalem (Acts 20:22). Even though Paul's companions urged him to avoid the trouble surely waiting for him there, Paul committed to obey God and fulfill his ministry calling.

If you have time, read Acts 21:27–40; 22:1–30; and 23:1–10. These passages detail the desperate circumstances Paul faced in Jerusalem. If you don't have time the following bullet points will give you a quick overview to prepare you for the discussion and questions ahead.

- A Jewish mob seized Paul at the temple and tried to kill him.
- The uproar drew Roman soldiers who arrested Paul and put him in chains just in time to save his life.

- The soldiers carried Paul through the violent mob to get him safely to the barracks.
- The Roman commander gave Paul permission to speak to the crowd, but when he told them God sent him to take the gospel to the Gentiles the crowd erupted again.
- The Roman commander ordered Paul flogged but backed off immediately when Paul revealed he was a Roman citizen.
- The next day, Paul was brought before the Sanhedrin for a hearing but once again, the violence became so great, the commander was afraid Paul would be torn apart.
- Paul, bruised and battered, spent another night locked in the military barracks.

☞ Paul was severely beaten, arrested, and falsely accused. Night fell with Paul in Roman custody. Half of Jerusalem wanted him dead. What do you think Paul's state of mind might have been that night? What thoughts could have been running through his mind? What do you think he might have prayed?

Now read Acts 23:11. Check any of the following statements that correctly reflect this divine encounter.

❏ God worked to free Paul from prison.

❏ God left Paul in prison because it was part of God's plan for him to testify about Jesus in Rome.

❏ Jesus appeared to Paul in his time of need to not only encourage and strengthen him but to also reassure him that God was in control.

This incident began Paul's long journey to Rome—not as a free man, but as a prisoner of the Roman Empire. Charles Swindoll reflects on this nighttime visit in his book *Paul: A Man of Grit and Grace*:

> The Lord assured Paul of his continued safety. In addition, Rome would be his destination. What comfort that must have been to the man who, again, bore the marks of torturous treatment. Survival seems next to impossible, until the Lord intervenes. At that point, we realize He has a bigger plan than we could possibly have imagined. Often, in the midst of great pain, on the heels of mistreatment, the Lord appears in His Word, providing peace through His Spirit.

🕮 In what ways did God meet Paul's greatest need at that moment?

The next day, an organized plot to kill Paul was revealed, so the Roman commander secretly moved Paul under heavy guard to Caesarea. Held in Herod's palace, Paul gave testimony before governors and kings but was not released due to pressure from the Jewish leaders. After two years, when the Jews petitioned newly-appointed Governor Festus to transfer Paul back to Jerusalem for "trial," Paul appealed to Caesar. Under custody of a Roman centurion, Paul and his companions boarded a ship bound for Rome. The journey would not be uneventful.

Read Acts 27:13–26. Briefly describe the situation.

How did God demonstrate His sovereignty and grace to Paul? To the rest of the men?

📖 After a three-month delay on the island of Malta, Paul finally arrived in Rome. Read Acts 28:11–16, 30 and Philippians 2:25; 4:18. List all the ways you can find God graciously providing for Paul during his imprisonment in Rome.

Paul spent two years under house arrest in Rome while waiting for a hearing before Caesar. Under guard and confined to a regular house, Paul could receive visitors, but he also had to provide for his own needs. While Paul may have been able to do some work as a tent maker (Acts 18:3), the restrictions would have made it difficult to meet all his physical needs. God provided through the encouragement of local believers and gifts from the Christians in Philippi.

God did not release Paul from prison, calm the seas, or save the ship. Instead God gave Paul an anchor of grace that held him securely to our rock-solid God even while the storm raged on. God did not remove the difficult circumstances, but He graciously gave Paul everything he needed to keep going.

TEACHING IT

In 2 Corinthians, Paul wrote extensively about his suffering and the presence, power, and provision of the Holy Spirit in his life. In fact, God's sustaining grace poured out in suffering is a major theme in this letter.

Read 2 Corinthians 1:3–7. In verse 3, what phrases does Paul use to describe God?

In verses 3–7, how many times does Paul use either the noun or verb form of the word *comfort*?

The Greek noun translated as "comfort" in this passage is *paraklēsis*. According to *Vine's Complete Expository Dictionary*, *paraklēsis* means a "calling to one's side; an exhortation, or consolation, comfort." In John 14:16, Jesus used the masculine form of this noun, *paráklētos*, to refer to the Holy Spirit.

↳ Considering the definition of comfort and Paul's description in this passage, how does God comfort us when we suffer? In what ways can we receive His comfort?

In last week's lesson we learned how God works through our sufferings to strengthen and refine our faith. He never wastes our trials but uses them for our good. But His grace in our trials doesn't stop there. He comforts us in our struggles by the presence of His Spirit and through His people. God even uses our difficult experiences to benefit others.

According to 2 Corinthians 1:3–7, how does God use our suffering to help others?

Shared grief provides a unique form of comfort. Those with common experiences and pain know best how we sufferers feel and know what we need most. Those who have received God's comfort in a similar trial can extend that same comfort to us. In turn, when God comforts us, we are uniquely equipped to then comfort others. As we testify to God's strength and comfort to us, it builds their trust in God during their own times of suffering. Sharing our experience builds their faith.

☞ Briefly describe a time someone who experienced a trial similar to yours brought you comfort.

☞ Now think about times God has comforted you by the presence and power of His Holy Spirit. Is there someone you know today that would benefit from your experience? If yes, will you commit to reach out to them?

God may not change our difficult circumstances, but He will comfort us. He will draw us close to His side through the presence of His Spirit to encourage and console. He will ease our pain and grief through the fellowship of His people. Praise be to the God of all comfort!

Read 2 Corinthians 12:7–10, which we considered last week. How did Paul feel about the thorn in his flesh? What emotions and actions did it foster?

How did God answer Paul's prayer to remove the thorn?

God used Paul's thorn for good in his life. Paul could have easily become prideful over the "great revelations" he'd received, but the thorn kept pride at bay. Instead of removing the thorn, God gave Paul what he needed to endure and even rise above the thorn. God's strength met Paul's weakness. Paul's insufficiencies displayed God's all-sufficient grace.

Let's dwell for a moment on Paul's situation. For the sake of our discussion, let's assume Paul's thorn was a chronic illness. Over and over Paul asked God to heal him. Over and over God said "no" to healing but "yes" to grace.

↞ Brainstorm some ways God's grace could have been sufficient for Paul if he struggled with a chronic illness.

If Paul suffered from constant pain, God's grace would have given him what he needed to endure that pain. If Paul became so despondent he contemplated quitting the ministry, God's grace would have flooded his mind with peace and encouraged his heart. We don't know the specifics, but we do know the outcome. Where Paul was weak, God was strong.

Paul learned the power of weakness. He acknowledged his need to God and accepted God's strength. Paul pushed out pride and self-sufficiency and made room for the abundant flow of God's sufficient grace. The same will be true for us. What we lack in our weakness, God will provide by His grace.

In what areas of your life do you feel weak right now? Set aside your self-sufficiency and make room for God's strength. Write a prayer to God, acknowledging your need for His grace.

LIVING IT

When Emma married Jonathan they knew money would be very tight at first. Both still in college, their part-time jobs barely paid the bills. Some months there wasn't much money left for food.

They believed God could change their situation. They shared their need with a few close friends and their small group from church. They asked for prayer. The bills remained the same. Neither Emma nor Jonathan received a raise. The refrigerator and the bank account were almost empty. But God provided.

One afternoon Emma found an envelope in the mailbox without a postmark or a return address. Someone had driven by and dropped it off. The note was handwritten and short. It read, "Thought you could use this. Your friend."

Inside was a gift card for the local grocery store loaded with enough money to feed them until the next payday. The notes and gift cards continued regularly until Jonathan graduated and started his full-time job. God did not change their situation, but He graciously provided food through an unnamed friend.

Often, God graciously meets our needs through other people. His Spirit moves them to reach out, pray, or give. In the first section of this week's lesson, we learned that the believers in Philippi sent Epaphroditus to Rome to help meet Paul's needs while he was under house arrest. God can and will do the same for you.

🕊 Think about your own life. In what ways has God provided for your needs through other people?

The experience I told you about at the beginning of this lesson impacted me in multiple ways. First, anytime I am tempted to think God doesn't see my need or doesn't care, the Spirit brings this moment to mind. And I know, God does see me. He does care.

This experience also changed the way I respond to prompts by the Holy Spirit. The Spirit prompted my son-in-law to pray. Jeremy obeyed and God answered His prayer by filling me with peace. When the Spirit prompts me to pray for someone or urges me to call, send a card, or give something specific, it's because He wants to use me as a tool for His grace. I want to be a part of that!

☞ How have you responded to similar prompts in the past? Have you recognized these "prompts" as God's Spirit at work?

☞ Has the Spirit been prompting you to do something recently? If so, what is it? How will you obey?

When God doesn't change our circumstances, He still meets our needs in the midst of them. Sometimes He makes physical provision like the gift cards to Emma and Jonathan. But He always provides His presence, peace, and strength when we lean on Him.

Read Hebrews 4:14–16. Check any of the following statements that accurately reflect what the author of Hebrews encourages us to do "in our time of need." (Note: Many scholars believe Paul wrote Hebrews.)
❑ Abandon the faith we profess
❑ Confidently approach God's throne of grace
❑ Receive God's mercy and His grace

According to Hebrews 4:15, in what is Jesus uniquely equipped to comfort us?

☞ Read Philippians 4:10–13. What is the "context" of this passage? What situation prompts Paul to write these words?

This passage is often misused. We tend to pull verse 13 out of its original setting to claim Christ's strength for every endeavor—sometimes even our own purposes and goals. But here, Paul reflected on Christ's sustaining strength for him in times of need. No matter Paul's physical circumstances, he found total sufficiency in trusting Christ. Paul gained strength from Jesus to be content no matter his physical condition—in want or plenty.

Is there a situation in your life today in which you need Christ's strength? If so, approach His throne of grace with boldness today. Write a prayer below and ask God to strengthen you through His sustaining power.

GRACE APPLIED

After a long, seven-year battle, Courtney lost her mom Janet to a rare, incurable form of leukemia. Janet fought the cancer like she tackled everything else in her life, with tenacity and courage and unshakeable faith in her God.

From the beginning, Courtney believed Janet would beat the cancer. "Mom was always mentally strong, secure in her faith, and ran full speed tackling to-do lists and countless projects. She accomplished anything and everything she attempted. I didn't want to accept the probability we would lose her. I chose to think Mom would find a way to conquer this, too."

Courtney and Janet always had an especially close relationship. Courtney was an only child and Janet made the time to stay involved in her life. Even as Courtney married and began having children, she relied heavily on Janet for parenting advice, encouragement, and help. And Janet was always there to listen, pray, and pitch in.

But as the cancer slowly progressed, the relationship began to change. Physically, Janet could do less. Courtney became the encourager, the helper, and the intercessor. Through it all, Courtney expectantly waited for God's miraculous physical healing.

As Janet continued to deteriorate, Courtney spent more and more time with her. She read Scripture beside Janet's hospital bed. Courtney talked to her mom and prayed to the One who could heal her. Then very early on a warm summer morning, God took Janet home.

God did not answer Courtney's prayers for physical healing. Instead, He graciously answered her prayers in a much greater and eternal way. God healed Janet completely, thoroughly, and permanently. No more pain or chemo or blood transfusions.

But Courtney still lost her mother and friend. Courtney's three young children lost their Nana. How would God work in that?

Sadness marked the months that followed. But God also provided peace and comfort. Words of encouragement and consolation came through text messages, calls, e-mails, and cards. They ranged from family and close friends to acquaintances and even people Courtney had never met. Courtney recognized them all as an outpouring of God's grace through His people, a tangible expression of His presence with her.

"One particularly great source of comfort was a sweet friend who also lost her mom at an early age. She understood my hurt. Her encouragement came from like experience. I am so grateful she willingly revisited her own pain to ease mine."

Without Janet to lean on, Courtney began to seek more of God, to know Him like her mother had known Him. God worked through Janet's death to strengthen Courtney's faith and teach her more about Himself. Even in her grief, Courtney discovered that God is good and He is more than enough.

How did God answer Courtney's prayers for her mother?

Have you ever felt as though God didn't answer your prayers only to realize later He had answered in His more perfect way? If so, describe it.

How did God use other people to help Courtney in her grief?

Spend a few moments reflecting on a particularly difficult time of your life. Did you fail to recognize comfort and encouragement that came through other people as God's grace to you?

In what ways did God graciously work through the last difficult season of your life to bring about good for you and glory for Himself?

Week Nine: Glory of Grace
Grace Note: God graciously uses our trials as a testimony to others.

As I write this last week of study, ISIS rampages essentially unchallenged across the Middle East. ISIS soldiers blatantly hunt down Christians and continue to slaughter thousands in cruel and horrific ways.

The world watches and knows that many suffer because they claim Christ and refuse to reject Him. Their lives—and their deaths—testify to the Savior. Glory and grace overshadow murder and mayhem.

Eight weeks ago, when we first met Saul of Tarsus, he had a lot in common with these persecutors of Christians today. He passionately pursued Christians to arrest and even execute them. And like ISIS, Saul carried out this mission in the name of religion.

But God wooed Saul with His grace and lovingly intercepted him on the road to Damascus. God's grace saved, transformed, and called Saul the Pharisee to become Paul, the apostle of grace to the Gentiles.

Now, as we near the end of our journey with Paul, we will see his life come full circle. The persecutor becomes the persecuted. The one who witnessed the glory and grace of God on the face of Stephen becomes the one who exhibits them.

Two weeks ago, we considered God's purpose for our trials. We learned He uses the difficult circumstances of our lives to refine us spiritually and shape our character. Trials work our faith. Last week, we explored how God's grace sustains us in the midst of those trials. This week, we will discover another gracious aspect of a believer's trials: trials prove our faith works.

The world is always watching. When a believer—by God's sufficient grace—stands firm through suffering, there is no greater testimony to Christ. Paul's life—and death—testified to the grace, power, and faithfulness of God. God never wasted Paul's trials and sufferings. He graciously worked through them to bring honor and glory to Himself.

LEARNING IT

In last week's "Learning It" section, we left Paul under house arrest in Rome. Let's go back there now to see how God worked through Paul's "weaknesses" to bring glory to Christ.

Read Acts 28:16–31. Briefly describe Paul's encounter with Rome's Jewish leaders. In what ways was the gospel furthered and Christ glorified?

Reread Acts 28:30–31. In what other ways do you learn from these verses that the gospel was furthered and Jesus was glorified during Paul's Roman imprisonment?

Although we don't have a historical account of these two years, we aren't left completely without information. Scholars believe Paul penned four New Testament letters—Ephesians, Philippians, Colossians, and Philemon—during his Roman imprisonment. Paul may not have been able to leave his rented house, but we know from these letters and from Acts that Paul's ministry did not stop simply because he was in chains. He constantly shared the gospel with the lost who came to the house. He discipled visiting believers. He taught and encouraged the churches through his writing.

Read Colossians 4:7–18 and Philemon 1:23–24. How do these passages further develop our understanding of what Paul was doing while under house arrest?

Make a list of all the "fellow workers" Paul mentions in these passages who were with him in Rome. Now, beside their names, describe the different kinds of ministry and work they carried out.

Paul did not only evangelize, write, and teach during his two-year Roman imprisonment. He also continued his ministry to all the churches through his co-laborers for Christ. Picture that little rented house as a missions headquarters, constantly filled with people, activity, and prayer. The believers worked and studied together. Seekers and the curious came and went. And the Roman soldiers who guarded Paul day and night saw it all. As Paul dictated letters, as he shared the gospel message with spiritual seekers, and as Paul received reports from the churches, the soldiers were there.

In his book, *The Apostle: A Life of Paul*, John Pollock contemplates how God worked through this time of trial in Paul's life in a small, rented house in Rome:

In that Roman house, bitter people softened; anger, wrath, clamor died away. Paul had more than ever a sense of his littleness, his unworthiness—"less than the least of all saints"—and of the marvel of being entrusted with a commission "to preach the unsearchable riches of Christ." He seemed to delight in the contrast between the majesty of the message and the insignificance of the messenger: such a gentle little man now, yet with what steel and strength. The soldiers, turn and turn about, knew where that strength had its chief contact with infinity. In the early mornings, the guard chained to Paul had no option but to join the time on his knees and hear the words of thanksgiving and intercession.

Everyone who came into contact with Paul knew the source of his strength. He was quick to point to the sufficiency of God's grace and give Him all the glory. For instance, Paul wrote the following passage during his Roman imprisonment.

Read Ephesians 3:13–21. Knowing what you know, describe Paul's "sufferings for you" at the time he wrote these words.

↞ Based on Paul's prayer for the Ephesians, briefly list ways God must have graciously sustained Paul during this time.

Some scholars think Paul was executed in AD 62, but most believe he was released after two years. We can't be sure if he was tried and acquitted or simply released. According to Richard N. Longenecker in *The Ministry and Message of Paul*, the Roman government could not hold a prisoner indefinitely. By the end of two years, prisoners either had to be tried, found guilty and executed, or released.

Read Philippians 2:24 and Philemon 1:22. Based on these verses, what did Paul expect to happen at the end of the two years?

Scripture does not clearly tell us what happened to Paul after Luke's account in Acts ends. However, scholars combined clues from Paul's later epistles with church tradition and made some educated guesses. Many believe Paul continued traveling the world as an evangelist and perhaps even made it as far as Spain. Then after several years of freedom (roughly AD 63–67), Longenecker postulates Paul was rearrested and ultimately beheaded under the Roman emperor Nero.

We have traveled a long way with Paul over these last nine weeks. Our study of the apostle of grace would not be complete without reading his last preserved written words. Scholars believe Paul wrote this second letter to his "son" Timothy from a dungeon in Rome, not long before his expected execution by Nero.

🖎 Read 2 Timothy 4:6–8. Rewrite this passage in your own words.

Had Paul's life of faith been easy?
Circle one: Yes   No

🖎 Based on everything you've learned in this study, how was Paul able to remain faithful to God's call for his life even to death?

🖎 Now write a brief statement to describe how Paul's suffering and trials pointed others to Jesus and gave Him glory.

Am I the only one who got emotional reading Paul's last words to Timothy? Paul held nothing back in his service to his Lord. Paul did not seek suffering and persecution, but he refused to disobey God in order to avoid it. His physical scars testified to the grace of Christ. Paul gave everything. But he received even more. Abundant grace, lavishly poured out.

TEACHING IT

Paul spent his life taking the gospel message to the lost no matter the cost. As a result, he endured tremendous suffering. Have you ever wondered why he did it? Why did he continue to preach and evangelize when he knew more pain was likely? One of Paul's letters to the believers in Corinth sheds some light on this question. Additionally, *The NIV Application Commentary* by Scott J. Hafemann expounds upon the context and culture of Corinth and the Corinthian church.

The Corinthian culture valued pleasure, status, wealth, and influence. In this city filled with a wide range of idols, the citizens chose to "worship" the god with the greatest potential to give them these things. Not surprisingly, false teachers had infiltrated the Corinthian church with a "gospel" that "promised them deliverance from suffering and a steady diet of spiritual experiences." In order to win them over, they had to undermine Paul's apostleship and authority over the Corinthian church. Paul's letter strongly implies they had cited Paul's suffering as evidence against him.

Read 2 Corinthians 4:5–15. Based on verse 5, which of the following statements reflect Paul's ministry and preaching? Check all that apply.

❑ Paul praised his own works and worthiness.

❑ Paul preached about the glory and greatness of Jesus.

❑ Paul ministered as a servant and did not seek to be served.

Paul's gospel message focused on this amazing truth: Jesus Christ— the glory of God—comes to dwell within us. The God of all creation makes His home in frail humans. And the presence of the Light dispels our darkness.

🕭 According to verse 7, what does this "treasure in jars of clay" reveal to others?

🕭 In verse 8–9, Paul gives four contrasts from his life that illustrate this truth. List the four "weakness" in the left column with the corresponding demonstration of God's power on the right.

PAUL'S WEAKNESS	GOD'S POWER

Our human weakness, our frailty, serves to magnify the glorious power of God. When we are not able to stand on our own, God's grace and strength are displayed. Every time a believer "faces death" by experiencing a trial or enduring pain, God intervenes and the life of Jesus is revealed through us.

Read 2 Corinthians 4:13–15. Paul's unwavering faith in the gospel message of Christ motivated his preaching. He could not remain silent about the salvation of Jesus and the guaranteed future resurrection of believers. According to verse 15, how did God use the ministry of this "weak" apostle?

God used Paul's preaching and his life of suffering for a great purpose. First, the believers in Corinth, as well as other believers who knew of Paul, were encouraged by the display of God's power in Paul's life. Second, the testimony of this "treasure in jars of clay" pointed many to salvation through the grace of God. And finally, both of these caused many to glorify God.

🖎 Based on what you've learned in this lesson, as well as other lessons, why didn't Paul give up? Why did Paul continue to take the gospel of Christ to the world when he knew more suffering was likely?

LIVING IT

As I finish writing this last week of study, our family is in a very stressful time. My 88-year-old father-in-law, who lives with us, is in the hospital being treated for a dangerous infection. At the same time, my brother and I are beginning the process of moving our parents out of their home of 45 years into an assisted living facility. My father's physical health is declining rapidly and my mother's dementia has worsened to the point they can't continue to live independently.

A couple of days ago, when I was cleaning throw up from a sick dog off the beige rug, the pressure of all of this threatened to overwhelm me. How ironic! I've been studying and writing about the power of God's grace in a believer's life to sustain and strengthen us. And yet, in that moment, I forgot. I wasn't sure how to find what I needed to keep going.

Maybe that's you, too. Perhaps right now your life is filled with trials and difficulties and you need to know how to keep going. Let's go back to 2 Corinthians 4 and seek to apply Paul's experience to our own lives.

Paul finished this portion of his letter by summarizing both how and why he didn't lose heart over the sufferings he experienced. He readily admitted that the persecution and trials took a lasting physical toll, but they were nothing compared to the eternal glory that awaited him.

↦ Read 2 Corinthians 4:16–18. In the midst of his physical weakness, what did God do daily for Paul?

Even if our trials and struggles cause us to "waste away physically," God works in them by His grace and power to grow and strengthen us spiritually. Even the knowledge of this truth should encourage us.

Read Romans 5:3–5. Since we know God uses our sufferings for our good, what can we experience in the midst of them?

↦ Now, look back at 2 Corinthians 4:16–18. According to verse 18, what did Paul purposefully do when he faced trials?

Our pain and suffering rarely feel "light and momentary" when we are in the middle of them. Since we currently reside in this physical world, it's easy to allow physical things to overwhelm us. Yet, compared to what waits for us, even the worst of this life dims in light of the glorious reality of eternity. We must follow Paul's example and purposefully focus on the spiritual and eternal over the physical and temporary.

🖝 Make a list of everything you can think of that will help you follow Paul's example, purposefully focusing on the spiritual and eternal over the physical and temporary.

Sweet sister, God's grace is more than sufficient for your current trial and for any that lay ahead. His strength will be displayed in your weakness. Your trials will prove to everyone around you that faith in Jesus Christ works.

    As we near the end of our study together, let's focus in on this truth: God can and will use your suffering to point others to Jesus. Paul experienced this. In his letter to the believers in Philippi, Paul wrote about how God used his imprisonment in Rome to advance the gospel.

🖝 Read Philippians 1:12–14 and 18b–21. In what ways did God use Paul's imprisonment?

🖝 Because of what God had and would accomplish, what was Paul's attitude regarding his suffering?

Now think about your own trials and difficulties. Are you willing to allow God to use your life in whatever way will bring Him the most honor and glory? If so, write a prayer expressing that feeling. If you aren't at a point where you can honestly pray that, write a prayer asking God to make His purposes for your life more important than your comfort.

GRACE APPLIED

About six months ago, my precious sister-friend Janet lost her battle with cancer. At the end of last week's lesson you read about Janet's daughter, Courtney, and how God sustained her with His grace through the loss of her mother. I dedicated this book to Janet because she taught me so much about God's lavish grace.

Janet's life exemplified the sufficiency and power of God's grace. Her "weakness" constantly revealed God's glory and strength. She gave God the glory and praised the name of Jesus every step of the way. In small victories and massive setbacks, she stood firm, unshakeable in her resolve to hold tight to her Savior. And I had a front row seat to God's grace poured out in Janet's life.

In 2008, Janet was diagnosed with myelofibrosis, a rare form of leukemia. She participated in a number of clinical trials. She endured regular chemo. She was in and out of the hospital, increasingly so the last couple of years. Although Janet had days of discouragement and days she wanted to give up, those days were the exception. Overall, Janet clung tightly to God and shared Jesus with everyone who would listen.

In the last few weeks of her life, the doctors also treated Janet for a fungal infection in her lungs. The aggressive treatment required almost daily trips to the hospital for intravenous medications. Many of Janet's friends, including me, pitched in to help her husband with the hospital trips, which often took all day. I wanted to help and encourage her, but she blessed me instead.

On one trip, the lab tech struggled to get the blood she needed for testing from Janet's port. Getting it from another vein would have been an ordeal. Janet naturally went straight to prayer. Not silent prayer, but out loud, asking God to intervene. The lab tech and I both joined in. Within moments the blood was flowing and the three of us were singing a praise chorus.

On another day, during yet another intravenous treatment, I walked with her down the hallway to the bathroom, as she pushed the IV pole ahead of her. I stood outside the bathroom door, just in case she needed anything. When I heard her voice I asked if she was OK. She quickly replied, "Yes. I'm just talking to Jesus."

God used the crucible of this terrible illness to refine Janet's faith and foster total dependency on Him. Her relationship with Jesus was intimate and real and very tangible. Anyone she came into contact with could feel it, even if they didn't understand it. She never hesitated to tell others the source of her strength.

Janet's journey greatly impacted me. I watched her faith grow increasingly stronger even as her body grew weaker. She leaned on God every moment. She gave Him praise for everything, big and small. She never hesitated to talk about Jesus with the medical personnel, hospital employees, and other patients. Her trust in God and her love for Jesus were obvious. Her physical weakness revealed the strength and grace of God.

God's grace was sufficient for Janet (2 Corinthians 12:9). When "hard pressed on every side," she demonstrated God's "all-surpassing power" (2 Corinthians 4:7). She knew her "light and momentary troubles" would soon give way to eternal glory (2 Corinthians 4:17). And she shared that sure hope with everyone.

Janet's trials worked her faith. And to everyone who watched, Janet's trials proved her faith worked. Janet's life—and death—pointed others to the grace and glory of God.

In what ways did Janet's illness demonstrate the grace and faithfulness of God?

How did her "weakness" reveal God's power?

Has there ever been a time in your life when God worked through a trial or difficulty to point others to Jesus? If so, describe it.

If you are not in a time of difficulty now, you probably will be in the future. List ways you can purposefully allow God to use your life as a testimony of grace to others.

CLOSING WORDS

Sweet friend, thank you for allowing me to lead you in this discovery of God's lavish grace. I pray God will continue to pour out, pour through, and overflow His grace into your life. May His grace be more than sufficient for you today and every day. "The grace of the Lord Jesus Christ be with your spirit. Amen" (Philippians 4:23).

LEADER'S GUIDE

Dear Leader,

Whether this is your first time to lead a small group or you've done it dozens of times, this journey will be unique. God has chosen you to lead this specific group of women through this specific material at this specific time. That is His grace working in your life—and theirs.

As I studied about the Apostle Paul and God's lavish grace, I thought of you. Every time God overwhelmed me with fresh insight or I rejoiced over a new understanding of a facet of His grace, I anticipated the moment that God would also show those things to you. May God flood your heart with gratitude and stretch your faith to new levels in the weeks ahead.

Before you get started, read the study introduction for an explanation of the way the study is organized. Feel free to use the suggestions in this guide or adapt them as God leads. You know the specific needs of the women in your group. However, consider these general suggestions:

• As you complete each week of study, use a highlighter to mark questions or statements that are particularly relevant to you or your group. Include these in your small group time.

- Find the "Grace Note" statement at the beginning of each week. This statement summarizes the primary truth of each week's lesson. Keep this in mind as you prepare and lead your group.

- Look for the questions marked by the special icons. These questions are particularly suitable for group discussion and focus on main points or foundational truths.

- Leave time each week to read the "Grace Applied" story and ask the follow-up questions. These real-life stories will help your group members see how the biblical truths can apply to their lives.

- Focus on application as much as possible. Help your group members make the connection between the biblical principles and their lives today.

The following suggestions for each week's group time are just that—suggestions. Feel free to come up with your own opening activity or discussion question.

OPTIONAL INTRODUCTORY WEEK

If you meet with your group before they've had a chance to do homework, feel free to use the following suggestions for your time together.

1. Introductory discussion: How would you define "grace"? How have you heard "grace" defined? Is there a difference between grace that God extends and grace that we extend? When does God extend His grace to us?

2. Ask your group to turn to page 27 and read through the definition of *chàris*, the Greek word translated as "grace" in the New Testament.

3. Guide discussion on the meaning of grace. If you have time and access to word study tools, dig deeper into the meaning of *chàris*. Ask: In what ways does the definition of *chàris* expand your understanding of grace? Did anything surprise you?

4. Hand out the Bible study books.

5. Refer your group to the book's introduction. Walk through how the book is put together by pointing out the three main parts and the four sections within each week.

6. Ask: How do you expect God to use this study of His Word in your life?

WEEK ONE

1. Ask: Have you ever misunderstood or underestimated God's grace? If so, in what ways?

2. Read Charles Swindoll's quote in the "Learning It" section. Discuss Saul's feelings and attitudes about the growth of the Christian "cult."

3. Discuss the questions marked with the icon in the "Learning It," "Teaching It," and "Living It" sections.

4. Summary discussion question: Based on Saul's life before salvation and his later writings, how would Saul describe the role of God's grace in his salvation?

5. Ask: Has this lesson helped you gain a new understanding of the role of God's grace in your life before you were saved? If so, in what ways?

6. Read the "Grace Applied" story and discuss the questions that follow the story.

WEEK TWO

1. Ask your group to give a thorough description of Saul before salvation. Use the first question in "Learning It" to help.

2. Use Acts 9:1–19 as a script for a brief play. Assign roles to members of your group or ask for volunteers. Encourage them to improvise and be dramatic. Some may feel this is a bit awkward, but the group could have fun with it! Here are the suggested parts:
   • Narrator
   • Saul
   • High Priest
   • Saul's traveling companions
   • Jesus
   • Ananias

3. Read Acts 26:12–14 from Saul's testimony before King Agrippa. Then ask this: How does Jesus' metaphor about "kicking against the goads" describe God's grace at work in Saul's life?

4. Read 1 Timothy 1:12–17 and Charles Swindoll's quote on page 38. Ask: Why do you think Paul has been called "the apostle of grace"?

5. Discuss the questions marked with the icon in this week's "Teaching It" section.

6. Don't assume everyone in your group has a saving relationship with Jesus. "Walk down" the Roman road as a group and discuss. (Use the first question marked with the icon in the "Living It" section.) Make yourself available to talk after class.

7. Read the "Grace Applied" story and discuss the questions that follow the story.

WEEK THREE

1. As a group, review what God saved us "from." Refer to Ephesians 2:1–22 and the chart you completed in last week's "Teaching It" section if you need help.

2. Read this week's "Grace Note" and ask the group to describe how a believer's purpose, ministry, and spiritual growth are works of God's grace.

3. Use the questions marked with the icon in this week's "Learning It" section to guide a discussion of the following:
   • God's unique purpose for Saul
   • How God used Saul's background for His purposes
   • How Saul/Paul carried out that purpose

4. Discuss the questions marked with the icon in this week's "Teaching It" section.

5. Ask for volunteers from the group to share what they learned about their own place of service and ministry in this week's "Living It" section.

6. Read 1 Timothy 4:7–8 and Titus 2:11–15. Discuss with your group how a believer's spiritual growth is a joint-effort between the believer and the working of God's grace through the ministry of the Holy Spirit.

7. Read the "Grace Applied" story and discuss the follow-up questions.

WEEK FOUR

1. Ask: How did God's grace transform Nicky Cruz? How did Nicky then extend God's grace to others? Have you ever known someone whose life was radically transformed by God's grace? In what ways did they extend it to others?

2. Take your group back to first century Jerusalem. Ask them to describe how the believers probably felt about Saul and why. Ask them to share how they would have responded when Saul showed up claiming to be a Christian.

3. Discuss Barnabas's treatment of Saul from the question marked with the icon in this week's "Learning It" section.

4. Read Ephesians 1:1–8. Have your group use the information in this passage to describe the "unbounded" nature of God's

grace. Ask: What are we to do with the abundance of grace God gives us?

5. Read Ephesians 4:29 and the definitions of the Greek words Paul used to describe our speech.

6. Ask: What is the result of corrupt speech? What is the result of gracious speech?

7. Optional object lesson: Bring a beach ball to class and use it to demonstrate the effects of corrupt speech and gracious speech as described in the lesson. Ask your group to shout out examples of corrupt speech while you deflate the ball. Then ask your group to give examples of gracious speech while you blow air into the ball.

8. Read Matthew 12:33–37 and discuss how our words directly reflect what's in our hearts. Use the list on page 74 to kick off a discussion of ways we can foster gracious overflow.

9. Read the "Grace Applied" story and answer the questions that follow it.

WEEK FIVE

1. Ask: What does the world teach us about how to treat others? What characteristics often mark worldly relationships?

2. Read this week's "Grace Note." Ask: How does grace make it possible for a believer to relate to others differently than the world relates to others?

3. Discuss the question marked with the icon in this week's "Learning It" section.

4. Prompt your group to think of some contemporary situations that compare to the situation in Philemon. Ask: How could these situations be handled with grace?

5. Read the definition of *agapé* on page 86. Ask: How is *agapé* different from the way the world loves?

6. Read Ephesians 5:21. Now read the definition for *submit* on page 87. Ask the group to describe in practical ways what it means to willingly submit ourselves to someone else.

7. Discuss the question marked with the icon in this week's "Teaching It" section.

8. Discuss the questions marked with the icon in this week's "Living It" section.

9. Read the "Grace Applied" story and the questions that follow it.

WEEK SIX

1. Ask your group to share instances when their ungracious behavior negatively impacted the name and reputation of Jesus. (Note: Remind your group to use discretion in what they share.)

2. Discuss the questions marked with the icon in this week's "Learning It" sections.

3. Read Galatians 3:1–5 and 5:1–6. Now reread 5:4. Ask: Why did Paul say that Gentile believers who were circumcised had "fallen away from grace"? What are some "good works" that pull Christians today "away from grace"?

4. Ask: In what ways was circumcision for Timothy different than circumcision for the average Gentile believer?

5. Briefly review the two examples of Paul's witnessing encounters we read in Acts 17 and 26. Read my bulleted list of gracious characteristics and bridge-building methods on page 103. Ask your group to share anything else they discovered in the passages or any other gracious characteristics and bridge-building methods they have seen or used.

6. Discuss the questions marked with the icon in this week's "Teaching It" section.

7. Ask: What does it mean to share the gospel with both grace and truth? What does it look like?

8. Discuss the questions marked with the icon in this week's "Learning It" section.

9. Read the "Grace Applied" story and the questions that follow it.

WEEK SEVEN

1. Open this week's discussion by reading the quote from Charles Swindoll on page 121. Ask: How does this compare to what you've heard about trials in the lives of believers?

2. Have your group call out as many of Paul's trials and difficulties they can remember. Ask: How do you think you would have responded to all this if you were Paul?

3. Discuss the questions marked with the icon in this week's "Learning It" section.

4. Read Romans 5:1–5; James 1:2–4; and 1 Peter 1:6–7. Have the group describe how God uses trials to "work" our faith.

5. Discuss the questions marked with the icon in this week's "Living It" section.

6. Read the "Grace Applied" story and the questions that follow it.

WEEK EIGHT

1. Review last week's "Grace Note" with your group to prepare them for this week's discussion. Ask: Why does God sometimes allow trials and difficulties into our lives? In what ways does He use them?

2. Now read this week's "Grace Note." Ask your group to share examples from their own lives.

3. Summarize for your group the events in Jerusalem described in Acts 21:27–40; 22:1–30; and 23:1–11. (Feel free to ask a volunteer to do this!)

4. Discuss the questions marked with the icon in this week's "Learning It" section.

5. Read 2 Corinthians 1:3–7 and 12:7–10. Discuss the questions marked with the icon in this week's "Teaching It" section.

6. Discuss the questions marked with the icon in this week's "Living It" section.

7. If you have time to go deeper, reread Philippians 4:10–13 and lead a discussion on taking a passage out of biblical context. The following two posts will help:
   • kathyhoward.org/do-you-misuse-philippians-413
   • kathyhoward.org/biblical-context-4-things

8. Read the "Grace Applied" story and the questions that follow it.

WEEK NINE

1. Ask your group to explain this statement: "Trials prove our faith works."

2. Ask your group to describe Paul's life and ministry during his two-year Roman imprisonment based on what they learned this week in the "Learning It" section.

3. Ask the first question marked with the icon in this week's "Learning It" section.

4. Review Paul's probable history during the years AD 62–67 with your class.

5. Discuss the remaining three questions marked with the icon in the "Learning It" section.

6. Use the material in the lesson to set the stage for the situation in Corinth when Paul wrote 2 Corinthians.

7. Read 2 Corinthians 4:5–15 and discuss the questions marked with the icon in this week's "Teaching It" section.

8. Discuss the questions marked with the icon in this week's "Living It" section.

9. Read the "Grace Applied" story and the questions that follow it.

New Hope® Publishers is a division of WMU®, an international organization that challenges Christian believers to understand and be radically involved in God's mission. For more information about WMU, go to wmu.com. More information about New Hope books may be found at NewHopePublishers.com. New Hope books may be purchased at your local bookstore.

Use the QR reader on your
smartphone to visit us online at
NewHopePublishers.com

If you've been blessed by this book, we would like to hear your story. The publisher and author welcome your comments and suggestions at: newhopereader@wmu.org.

More New Hope Bible Studies for Women

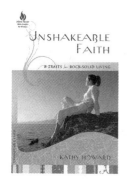

Unshakeable Faith
KATHY HOWARD
ISBN-13: 978-1-59669-297-8 • $8.99

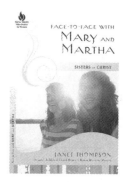

Face-to-Face with Mary and Martha
JANET THOMPSON
ISBN-13: 978-1-59669-254-1 • $8.99

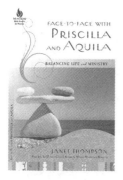

Face-to-Face with Priscilla and Aquila
JANET THOMPSON
ISBN-13: 978-1-59669-295-4 • $8.99

Face-to-Face with Naomi and Ruth
JANET THOMPSON
ISBN-13: 978-1-59669-253-4 • $8.99

To see more studies from the "Face-to-Face" series,
visit NewHopePublishers.com.